The Best of
TAIWANESE CUISINE

HIPPOCRENE IS NUMBER ONE IN INTERNATIONAL COOKBOOKS

AFRICA AND OCEANIA
Best of Regional African Cooking
Egyptian Cooking
Good Food from Australia
Traditional South African Cookery
Taste of Eritrea

ASIA AND NEAR EAST
The Best of Taiwanese Cuisine
Imperial Mongolian Cooking
The Joy of Chinese Cooking
Healthy South Indian Cooking
The Indian Spice Kitchen
Best of Goan Cooking
Best of Kashmiri Cooking
Afghan Food and Cookery
The Art of Persian Cooking
The Art of Turkish Cooking
The Art of Uzbek Cooking

MEDITERRANEAN
Best of Greek Cuisine
Taste of Malta
A Spanish Family Cookbook
Tastes of North Africa

WESTERN EUROPE
Art of Dutch Cooking
Best of Austrian Cuisine
A Belgian Cookbook
Cooking in the French Fashion (bilingual)
Celtic Cookbook
Cuisines of Portuguese Encounters
English Royal Cookbook
The Swiss Cookbook
Traditional Recipes from Old England
The Art of Irish Cooking
Feasting Galore Irish-Style
Traditional Food from Scotland
Traditional Food from Wales
The Scottish-Irish Pub and Hearth Cookbook
A Treasury of Italian Cuisine (bilingual)

SCANDINAVIA
Best of Scandinavian Cooking
The Best of Finnish Cooking
The Best of Smorgasbord Cooking
Good Food from Sweden

CENTRAL EUROPE
All Along the Rhine
All Along the Danube
Best of Albanian Cooking
Best of Croatian Cooking
Bavarian Cooking
Traditional Bulgarian Cooking
The Best of Czech Cooking
The Best of Slovak Cooking
The Art of Hungarian Cooking
Hungarian Cookbook
Art of Lithuanian Cooking
Polish Heritage Cookery
The Best of Polish Cooking
Old Warsaw Cookbook
Old Polish Traditions
Treasury of Polish Cuisine (bilingual)
Poland's Gourmet Cuisine
Taste of Romania
Taste of Latvia

EASTERN EUROPE
The Best of Russian Cooking
Traditional Russian Cuisine (bilingual)
The Best of Ukrainian Cuisine

AMERICAS
Argentina Cooks
Cooking the Caribbean Way
Mayan Cooking
The Honey Cookbook
The Art of Brazilian Cookery
The Art of South American Cookery
Old Havana Cookbook (bilingual)

The Best of
TAIWANESE CUISINE

Recipes and Menus for Holidays and Special Occasions

by Karen Hulene Bartell

HIPPOCRENE BOOKS INC.
NEW YORK

Paperback edition, 2002
Copyright© 2001 Karen Hulene Bartell.

Book and jacket design by Acme Klong Design.

For information, address:
Hippocrene Books, Inc.
171 Madison Avenue
New York, NY 10016

Library of Congress Cataloging-in-Publication Data

Bartell, Karen H.
    The best of Taiwanese cuisine : recipes and menus for holidays and
special occasions / by Karen Hulene Bartell.
        p.   cm.
      ISBN 0-7818-0855-3 hb; 0-7818-0950-9 pb
      1. Cookery, Chinese. 2. Cookery--Taiwan. 3. Holiday cookery--Taiwan.
    4. Menus. I. Title: Taiwanese cuisine. II. Title.

    TX724.5.C5 B37 2001
    641.595124'9--dc21   2001024740

Printed in the United States of America.

This is dedicated to Hei Mao, with special thanks to my husband Peter and Tai Ji, who conspired to make my five years in Taiwan enjoyable ones.

A note of gratitude to the University of Texas and the Perry-Castaneda Library for allowing the reproduction of the map of Taiwan.

Table of
CONTENTS

Introduction to
TAIWAN

 **GEOGRAPHY.** Shaped like a sweet potato, Taiwan is located in the Pacific Ocean about 100 miles from the southeastern coast of China. Roughly 250 miles long and 90 miles wide at its broadest point, the island is midway between Korea and Japan to the north and the Philippines and Hong Kong to the south. Taiwan is a natural gateway to Asia.

It is also a cultural transition to the Orient. Distinctly Eastern but increasingly Westernized, Taiwan is firmly lodged between the Orient and the Occident. Known to the early Portuguese sailors as Ilha Formosa, or the Beautiful Island, Taiwan is largely urbanized now. Sub-tropical forests still exist in the Central Mountain Range, but the island is heavily developed and industrialized.

BACKGROUND. Taiwan has been called the Republic of China (ROC) since 1949, when Communists of the People's Republic of China (PRC) defeated the Nationalist Chinese army. Chiang Kai-shek's forces retreated from the Chinese mainland to build a provisional capital in Taipei, Taiwan. The official language is Mandarin Chinese, and English is increasingly heard, but Taiwanese is still the prevalent language. Taoism and Buddhism are the main religions, and because the philosophy of Confucianism is also respected, education is highly valued.

Taiwan may rightly be called the citadel of Chinese culture, adhering strictly to ancient Chinese traditions, customs, written language, and cuisine. The National Palace Museum houses the largest collection of Chinese artifacts outside of the mainland, and certainly the many restaurants and teahouses are testaments to the culinary legitimacy of this island nation.

TAIWANESE CUISINE. Food holds an extremely important place in Taiwanese society. After polite greetings are exchanged, the first question a host or hostess asks guests is, "Have you eaten?" With this emphasis placed on hospitality, it is not surprising that the culinary arts have reached such a high level of sophistication.

Dishes from the four corners of China are found in Taiwanese kitchens and restaurants. Northern Chinese cuisine from Peking, Honan, and Mongolia depends on wheat, corn, peanuts, and soybeans, rather than rice, making noodles, breads, and dumplings popular items. Eastern cuisine from Shanghai and Soochow makes use of seafood, sauces, and herbs. Western-style cuisine from Szechuan, Hunan, and

Yunnan is well known for its spicy hot seasoning and fried foods. Southern Chinese cooking from Chaochow and Fukien include lightly seasoned, fresh seafood.

The following menus and recipes are all authentic renditions of foods found in Taiwan. Although dozens, if not hundreds, of various Chinese cooking styles are used in Taiwan, the Fukien recipes and methods of cooking are the most prevalent since the majority of Taiwanese are descendents from the Fukien Province of Mainland China.

PAPER CUTTING. Interspersed throughout the following pages of recipes are paper cuttings. They are one of the most popular Chinese folk arts, dating from the sixth century. Used for religious, ceremonial, and decorative purposes, paper cuttings decorate doors, mirrors, walls, windows, lamps, and lanterns.

At holidays and festivals, particularly Lunar New Year, paper cuttings abound. They're sold on every street corner and decorate many of the New Year cards. Doorways are decorated with paper cuttings for good luck. The favorite motif for New Year is the zodiac's animal of the year, for instance, dragons in the Year of the Dragon. For weddings and anniversaries, the preferred design is the symbol of Double Happiness, and for birthdays it is the character for Long Life.

In times past, all girls learned the art of paper cutting. Brides, in fact, were judged by their artistic abilities. Nowadays, it is professional artists, primarily males, who cut the paper by hand. Machines are never used for the intricate cuttings. Sharp knives or scissors are used to cut through the very fine rice or tissue paper, with up to eight fragile sheets of paper stacked together at a time.

Hopefully the paper cuttings will add the flavor of the Taiwanese culture to the cuisine and enhance your cookery experience.

Winter:
LUNAR NEW YEAR

Lunar New Year, or Chinese New Year, as it is sometimes known in the United States, occurs in January or February, on the first day of the first month of the lunar year. It is the most important celebration in Asia. In Taiwan, schools close for several weeks, as they do in the United States for Christmas vacation. Businesses hold dinner parties for employees and distribute bonuses. Parents and grandparents give children red envelopes of "lucky money" called *hong bao*. Another New Year custom is buying and wearing new clothes to represent a new beginning. Red is the color of choice because it is believed to bring good luck. All debts must be paid off, and the house must be cleaned from ceiling to floor, so that the evil spirits of the past year are swept away. Fireworks are set off to chase evil spirits away from the next year. However, the most important tradition of all includes families and friends getting together to talk, laugh, feast, and celebrate the New Year.

According to Chinese mythology, the lunar calendar is a zodiac, with each year being represented by a different animal in a cycle of twelve.

LUNAR ZODIAC CALENDAR

RAT	1912	1924	1936	1948	1960	1972	1984	1996	2008
OX	1913	1925	1937	1949	1961	1973	1985	1997	2009
TIGER	1914	1926	1938	1950	1962	1974	1986	1998	2010
RABBIT	1915	1927	1939	1951	1963	1975	1987	1999	2011
DRAGON	1904	1916	1928	1940	1952	1964	1976	1988	2000
SNAKE	1905	1917	1929	1941	1953	1965	1977	1989	2001
HORSE	1906	1918	1930	1942	1954	1966	1978	1990	2002
RAM	1907	1919	1931	1943	1955	1967	1979	1991	2003
MONKEY	1908	1920	1932	1944	1956	1968	1980	1992	2004
ROOSTER	1909	1921	1933	1945	1957	1969	1981	1993	2005
DOG	1910	1922	1934	1946	1958	1970	1982	1994	2006
PIG	1911	1923	1935	1947	1959	1971	1983	1995	2007

SOLAR TERMS

Besides the lunar-calendar divisions, each year is classified into 24 solar phases. The terms are far more poetic than simply the names of the months. Closely related to nature, they lyrically describe the changing seasons. Reliant on the lunar calendar, all dates are approximate.

SOLAR TERM	CORRESPONDING DATE
Beginning of Spring	New Year's Day, February 5
Rain Water	Rainy season begins, February 19 to 20
Waking of Insects	Earth awakens, March 5
Spring Equinox	Solar Equinox, March 20 to 21
Pure Brightness	April 5
Grain Rain	Farmer's Almanac, April 20 to 21
Beginning of Summer	May 5
Grain Full	May 20 to 21
Grain in Ear	June 5
Summer Solstice	June 20 to 21
Slight Heat	July 6 to 7
Great Heat	July 22 to 23
Beginning of Autumn	August 7 to 8
Limit of Heat	August 23 to 24
White Dew	September 7 to 8
Autumn Equinox	September 22 to 23
Cold Dew	October 8 to 9
Frost's Descent	October 23 to 24
Beginning of Winter	November 7 to 8
Slight Snow	November 22 to 23
Great Snow	December 7 to 8
Winter Solstice	December 22 to 23
Slight Cold	January 5
Great Cold	January 20 to 21

Lunar New Year's
SEAFOOD BRUNCH FOR EIGHT

Sashimi

California Roll

Four-Flavored Shrimp Sushi

Salmon Sushi

Chili Sesame Dipping Sauce

Oyster Omelets

Steamed Crab with Lotus Root

Rice Congee with Shrimp

Taiwanese Sweet Potatoes

Fruit Platter with Rabbit-Ear Apples

Chiayi Pumpkinseed Sesame Brittle

Because Taiwan is an island, enclosed by the Pacific Ocean and the Taiwan Strait, fresh seafood is plentiful. What better way to celebrate the New Year than with sashimi, shrimp, salmon, oysters, and crab? Oysters are only edible in the months containing the letter "R," for example, January, February, March, April, September, October, November, and December. Since Lunar New Year always occurs in January or February, oysters are in season, and yellowfin and bluefin tuna are at their peaks.

Sushi and Sashimi

Because Taiwan was under Japanese rule from 1895 to 1945, Taiwanese food has a pronounced Japanese influence. Sushi and sashimi are favorite finger foods at buffets. Although many Americans believe that sushi is raw fish, it is actually a rolled combination of rice, vegetables, hard-boiled eggs, and cooked fish, which is then sliced into colorful pinwheels of flavor. Raw fish is known as sashimi and is traditionally eaten at the beginning of the meal with ginger, *wasabi** and a dipping sauce. Sushi is eaten next, followed by the entrées.

Sashimi, made from the freshest cuts of raw fish** available, is easy to prepare. In fact, no cooking at all is necessary! Use shark, sea bass, cuttlefish, bonito, halibut, red snapper, lean yellowfin tuna, or bluefin tuna. This is best served in winter, when tuna is at its peak. Using a very sharp knife, simply cut boned, skinned fish fillets into bite-sized morsels (about 1 ^{1}/$_2$ inches long, 1 inch wide, and 1/4 inch thick) and serve on a chilled platter of greens. Garnish with pared ginger slices and slivers of green onions.

Sushi is almost as easy to make. Purchase a small mat made from bamboo sticks, called a *makisu*. On it, layer dried seaweed, known as *laver*, cooked rice (evenly spread), thin strips of carrots or cucumbers, and any combination of cooked fish, shellfish, or hard-boiled eggs. Be sure the layers are thin and even, and leave an extra bit of seaweed overlapping at the edge for securing. Roll up in a jellyroll fashion, pressing as you go. The seaweed, if pressed together, will seal itself. When set, slice it into pinwheel appetizers. Prepare several of the following recipes for a colorful display.

* *Wasabi* is a spicy-hot, green mustard sauce made with horseradish, available in Oriental grocery stores.

** Use every precaution in the preparation and eating of raw fish. Use only saltwater fish, not freshwater fish, which may contain parasites. Purchase the freshest fish possible from a reliable source, keep it refrigerated, and prepare it in a hygienic environment, making sure that hands, knives, and cutting surfaces are clean. When finished preparing the fish, wash hands, tools, and cutting surfaces in hot, soapy water.

CALIFORNIA ROLL

Dried seaweed
1 cup cooked rice
1/2 cup flaked cooked crabmeat
1 large avocado, thinly sliced
2 small cucumbers, sliced into thin strips, seeds removed

This easy-to-make sushi is popular with beginners. Jellyroll fashion, roll up the ingredients in the following order. Place the dried seaweed on top of a bamboo mat. Top with a thin layer of rice, followed by crabmeat, thin avocado slices, and finally 2 shoestring strips of cucumber for each roll. Roll tightly and slice into 4 pinwheels.
Makes 2 rolls or 8 slices.

FOUR-FLAVORED SHRIMP SUSHI

3 cups salted water
1 cup rice wine
1 green onion, sliced
1 tablespoon finely minced fresh ginger
8 prawns, cleaned, heads removed
1 lime, cut into 8 thin wedges

Combine salted water, wine, onion, and ginger. Bring to a boil, and add the prawns. Simmer for 5 to 6 minutes or until the prawns are opaque and cooked. Remove the shells, except for a small bit at the end of the tails. Butterfly the prawns and chill. Serve with *wasabi* and lime wedges.
Makes 8 servings.

SALMON SUSHI

Dried seaweed
1 cup cooked rice
1/2 cup thinly sliced smoked salmon or lox
1/2 small carrot, peeled, sliced into thin strips
1 small cucumber, sliced into thin strips, seeds removed

Jellyroll fashion, roll up the ingredients in the following order. Place the dried seaweed on top of a bamboo mat. Top with a thin layer of rice, followed by the salmon, and finally 2 shoestring-strips *each* of carrot and cucumber for each roll. Roll tightly and slice into 4 pinwheels.
Makes 2 rolls or 8 slices.

CHILI SESAME DIPPING SAUCE

1/4 cup soy sauce
1 tablespoon minced garlic
1/2 tablespoon rice vinegar
1/2 tablespoon raw or white sugar
1/2 tablespoon sesame oil
1/2 teaspoon minced chili pepper (to taste)

Combine ingredients well. Allow flavors to blend 1 hour at room temperature.
Makes about 1/2 cup sauce.

OYSTER OMELETS

Sesame oil is made from toasted sesame seeds. It has a distinctly nutlike flavor that enhances the taste of most Asian dishes.

4 eggs, beaten
Salt and pepper, to taste
4 fresh oysters, shelled, rinsed, and drained
1 tablespoon sesame oil

Mix the eggs, salt, and pepper with a fork. Stir in the oysters. Heat the oil in a 10-inch omelet pan or skillet. Pour in the oyster and egg mixture. Using a spatula, draw the cooked portions toward the center, tilting the mixture toward the edges of the skillet to hasten even cooking. When eggs are set and the oysters are done, fold and serve.
Makes 2 servings. Do not double recipe.

STEAMED CRAB WITH LOTUS ROOT

12 ounces fresh lotus root (purchase in Oriental grocery)
6 cloves garlic, minced
1 tablespoon minced fresh ginger
2 cups chicken or vegetable broth
2 crabs, cooked
1/4 teaspoon salt, or to taste
1/4 cup rice wine

Rinse the lotus root under running water, peel, and discard both ends. Slice root into 1/8-inch thick slices and place slices in water to prevent discoloration until root is completely sliced. Combine the first 4 ingredients in a large pot. Bring to a boil, then reduce the heat and simmer until the lotus roots are tender, about 10 minutes.

While the lotus roots simmer, open the crab shells, removed the gills, and rinse thoroughly. Remove the crab legs and claws. Crack the claws or cut in half. Cut the body of the crab into 4 pieces. Add the crab sections, legs, and claws, salt, and rice wine to the broth, and heat through, 5 to 10 minutes. Remove the crab and lotus root slices with a slotted spoon and serve on a platter.
Makes 8 servings.

RICE CONGEE WITH SHRIMP

Rice Congee is salty rice porridge, flavored with a bit of leftover meat or vegetables, or whatever else you might have on hand. It is as common a way to start the day in Taiwan as cornflakes or oatmeal are in the United States but with one big difference. The Taiwanese prefer salt, not sugar, to spice their morning meal.

Minced chicken, ham, shredded pork, or diced shiitake mushrooms may be substituted for the shrimp or presented in small bowls for self-service.

3 quarts chicken or vegetable stock
1 1/4 cups dry rice
1/2 teaspoon minced ginger
1/4 cup minced shrimp
1/4 cup finely sliced green onion

Bring the stock to a boil in a large pot. Add the rice and ginger. Simmer for 2 or 3 hours, stirring occasionally, so it does not stick. Add hot water if necessary. When the congee has the consistency of thin porridge, add the shrimp, if desired, or serve in a separate bowl, letting guests help themselves. Garnish with green onion slices.
Makes 8 cups.

TAIWANESE SWEET POTATOES

Not only is Taiwan shaped like a sweet potato, but the legumes were once a staple food of the island. Try Taiwan's modern preparation of this time-honored food: French-fried sweet potatoes.

METHOD I:

3 to 4 large sweet potatoes, peeled
2 cups vegetable oil for deep-frying
Ground white pepper, to taste

Slice the sweet potatoes into strips (as if for French fries). Deep-fry in oil until golden-brown and crispy. Dust heavily with pepper.
Makes 8 servings.

METHOD II:

Baking instead of deep-frying reduces the calories and cholesterol.

3 to 4 large sweet potatoes, peeled
1/4 cup sesame oil
Ground white pepper, to taste

Preheat oven to 350°. Slice the sweet potatoes into strips (as if for French fries). Shake the potato strips in a plastic bag with the oil to evenly coat each piece. Transfer the fries onto a greased baking sheet. Dust heavily with pepper, and bake, turning occasionally, for 30 minutes or until done.
Makes 8 servings.

FRUIT BOWL WITH RABBIT-EAR APPLES

1 pineapple
1 large honeydew melon
1 papaya, peeled, seeded, and cut into chunks
3 tangerines, peeled and sectioned
4 kiwis, peeled, sliced, and cut in half
2 tablespoons plus 1 teaspoon lime juice
1 apple, cored

 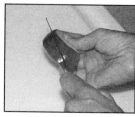 

Slice the pineapple lengthwise and discard the core. Reserving the "shells," cut pineapple into bite-sized chunks. Using a zigzag motion, cut the honeydew melon in a saw-tooth pattern. Reserving the "shells," seed and cut the honeydew into chunks. Combine all the ingredients (except the apple and 1 teaspoon of lime juice), tossing lightly, just until the lime juice evenly coats each morsel. Heap the fruit high in the hollow pineapple and honeydew halves.

Cut the apple in half, lengthwise. Cut each half into 4 horizontal slices. Cut into the peeling at the midpoint of each slice, creating an elongated "V." Carefully slice under the "V," between the peeling and the apple slice for 1 inch, making sure the skin is still firmly attached at the front base of the slice. Peel off the skin's back half of each slice. The "V" becomes the rabbit's ears, while the red apple peeling becomes the rabbit's face. Garnish the fruit bowl with the rabbit-ear apples.

Makes 8 servings.

CHIAYI PUMPKINSEED SESAME BRITTLE

1/4 teaspoon sesame oil
2 cups raw or light brown sugar
1/2 cup hulled green pumpkin seeds
1/4 cup sesame seeds

Line a cookie sheet with foil. Lightly grease the foil with sesame oil.
Caramelize the sugar in a heavy skillet by stirring with a fork over medium
heat until the sugar has melted and become a golden caramel. Be very careful
when working with hot candy! Remove the skillet from the heat, and add the
pumpkin and sesame seeds. Working quickly, pour the mixture onto the foiled
pan. After the brittle cools, break it into bite-sized pieces.
Makes 8 servings.

LUNAR NEW YEAR
Luncheon

Tea Eggs
Winter Melon Soup
Shrimp in Lettuce Cups
Cashew Beef with Egg Noodles
Stir-Fried Green Beans and Snow Peas
Pineapple Shortbread
Roasted Chestnuts
Tangerines

Because the family stays up late, feasting, watching fireworks, playing cards or Mahjong, talking, and lighting firecrackers at midnight, no one is prepared for an early breakfast. Excited children wake their parents for their *hong bao* or red envelopes of lucky money, and the day begins. Lunch is the first meal.

TEA EGGS

2 cups strong black tea
2 tablespoons raw or white sugar
4 hard-boiled eggs, shelled
4 cilantro sprigs
4 grape or cherry tomatoes

Combine the tea and sugar in a small container. Add the eggs, making sure they are submerged in the tea. Cover and refrigerate overnight. Drain the eggs, slice into colorful wedges, and present on a platter with cilantro sprigs and small tomatoes.
Serves 4.

WINTER MELON SOUP

One-half pound sliced button mushrooms may be substituted for the dried wood-ears. Do not soak them in hot water.

1/4 cup dried wood-ears mushrooms
2 cups hot water
1 1/2 pounds winter melon (available at Oriental markets)
1 quart chicken broth
1 cup coarsely chopped ham

Soak the dried mushrooms in the hot water for 30 minutes. Drain and slice. Peel the winter melon. Discard the seeds and stringy fibers. Cut the melon into 1-inch cubes (about 2 cups). Combine the mushrooms, melon, and broth in a 5-quart pot. Bring to a boil, lower heat, cover, and simmer for 12 to 15 minutes, or until the melon is tender. Serve in a tureen, and garnish with the chopped ham.
Serves 4.

SHRIMP IN LETTUCE CUPS

4 large, crisp center iceberg lettuce leaves
1 tablespoon minced green onions
1 tablespoon sesame oil
1 tablespoon rice vinegar
1/2 teaspoon salt, or to taste
1/4 teaspoon curry powder, or to taste
1/2 cup minced cooked shrimp
1/2 cup cooked, diced potatoes
1/4 cup cooked green peas
1/4 cup minced fresh mushrooms

Trim edges of lettuce by placing over the rounded side of a mixing bowl and cutting leaves into 4 neat "cups" with clean kitchen shears.

Mix the green onions, oil, vinegar, salt, and curry powder. Combine mixture with the shrimp, potatoes, peas, and mushrooms, tossing lightly to coat ingredients evenly. The mixture should be dry and crumbly.

Present the shrimp mixture in a bowl with a serving spoon. Place the 4 lettuce cups on a platter, and let people serve themselves. To eat, spoon the mixture into the cup, roll up, and eat out of hand like a taco.
Serves 4.

CASHEW BEEF WITH EGG NOODLES

EGG NOODLES

8 ounces Chinese egg noodles, cooked and drained
1/4 cup sesame oil
1/2 cup beef broth
1 tablespoon soy sauce, or to taste

Add noodles and sesame oil to a wok. Stir-fry for about 3 minutes, or until heated. Combine the broth and soy sauce. Pour it over the noodles, and stir-fry for 2 to 3 minutes, or until noodles are evenly coated. Remove to a heated platter.

CASHEW BEEF

1 pound rump steak
6 tablespoons sesame oil
1 tablespoon cornstarch
1 tablespoon soy sauce
1 tablespoon oyster sauce (prepared or see recipe page 82)
8 green onions, cut diagonally into 1-inch slices
1 minced chili pepper, optional
2 cloves garlic, minced
1 tablespoon minced fresh ginger
4 ounces unsalted, roasted cashews

Trim beef and slice across the grain into 1/4 x 2-inch slices. Heat 2 tablespoons of the oil in the wok, add half the beef, and stir-fry for 4 to 5 minutes, or until beef is browned. Transfer to a heated platter, and repeat with 2 tablespoons more of the oil.

Combine the cornstarch, soy sauce, and oyster sauce and set aside. Add 2 tablespoons oil, green onions, chili pepper, garlic, ginger, and cashews to the wok. Stir-fry for 1 minute, or until the onions are tender. Add the meat and cornstarch mixture. Stir-fry for 1 to 2 minutes, or until the sauce thickens. Spoon the cashew-beef mixture over the noodles and serve.
Serves 4.

STIR-FRIED GREEN BEANS AND SNOW PEAS

1 clove garlic, minced
1 tablespoon minced fresh ginger
2 tablespoons peanut or vegetable oil
1/2 cup vegetable or chicken broth
1 tablespoon soy sauce, or to taste
1/2 pound green beans, trimmed and sliced diagonally into 1/2-inch pieces
1/2 pound fresh snow peas, trimmed and strings removed
2 carrots, pared and sliced diagonally into 1/2-inch pieces
4 stalks celery, sliced diagonally into 1/2-inch pieces

Combine the garlic, ginger, and oil in a hot wok. Stir-fry for 1 minute. Add
the broth, soy sauce, and vegetables. Stir to coat, cover, and simmer vegetables
for 2 to 3 minutes, or until the carrots are crisp-tender.
Serves 4.

PINEAPPLE SHORTBREAD

Taiwanese bakeries make a rolled pineapple shortbread that is as chewy and yielding
as cake. Try purchasing the prepared pineapple shortbread in Oriental markets, or
make the following recipe, a crisp adaptation of the bakeries' secretly guarded recipe.

1 cup (2 sticks) butter
1/2 cup very fine sugar
2 cups sifted, all-purpose flour
3/4 cup (6 ounces) pineapple preserves

Preheat the oven to 300°. Cream the butter and sugar until light and airy,
about 3 minutes. Add the flour gradually, stirring until well blended.

Spread the dough evenly on an ungreased cookie sheet. Bake for 33 to 39 minutes, or until golden brown. Be careful not to scorch the edges. Remove the
cookie sheet from the oven, set it on a wire rack, and allow it to cool slightly.

When the shortbread is cool enough to handle but still malleable, spread it
with the pineapple preserves. Slice it lengthwise into 6 strips, and then cross-
wise into 9 strips to form 1-inch squares.
Makes about 54 squares.

LANTERN FESTIVAL
Dinner for Four

White Radish, Carrot, and Seaweed Salad
Corn Soup with Ginger
Three-Cups Chicken
Squash Stir-Fried with Rice Noodles
Bean Sprouts with Mustard Greens and Cilantro
Sweet Rice Dumplings (Tang Yuan)

Lantern Festival occurs on the first full moon following Lunar New Year. It marks the official end of the two-week holiday festivities. Traditionally, children made paper lanterns, placed candles inside, and then suspended them from long poles. At night the children would carry the lanterns before them, creating a parade.

Today in Taipei, families celebrate by attending the Lung Shan Temple to see children's paper lanterns, or they visit Chiang Kai-shek Memorial Hall to see the laser light show emanating from the immense lantern, which changes annually to represent the zodiac animal of the year. Afterward, they celebrate with families, friends, and good food.

Tang Yuan or Sweet Rice Dumplings are delicious balls of sticky rice filled with sweet or spicy centers that are traditional fare for the Lunar Lantern Festival. Their shape is round, symbolizing family unity. Find countless varieties of Tang Yuan in Oriental markets.

Create your own traditions! Decorate your dining room with strings of paper lanterns or candlelight. Make the meal festive with a centerpiece of mums and tiny paper umbrellas. Serve the meal with chopsticks and oversized soupspoons. (No cheating with forks or knives!) Prepare all or some of the following dishes for an unforgettable evening!

WHITE RADISH, CARROT, AND SEAWEED SALAD

1/2 cup dried, shredded seaweed (available at Oriental markets)
1/2 cup peeled, shredded white radish or daikon (available at Oriental markets)
1/2 cup peeled, shredded carrot
1/2 cup peeled, shredded cucumber
1/4 cup Plum Salad Dressing

Soak seaweed in water for 10 to 15 minutes. Remove and blanch in boiling water for 1 to 2 minutes. Remove, rinse under cold water, and drain thoroughly.

Divide the seaweed among 4 salad plates, mounding it in the center of each plate. Divide the white radish, carrot, and cucumber equally among the 4 plates, spooning each vegetable into a separate mound alongside the seaweed. Serve with Plum Salad Dressing (directions below).
Makes 4 servings.

PLUM SALAD DRESSING

6 tablespoons sesame oil
2 tablespoons rice wine vinegar, or white vinegar
1 tablespoon shredded, pitted, salted sour plums (available at Oriental markets)
1 teaspoon sugar, or to taste
Dash ground black pepper

Combine all ingredients, shake well in a covered container, and allow flavors to blend for at least 1 hour before serving with salad.
Makes 1/2 cup.

CORN SOUP WITH GINGER

1 can (15 ounces) creamed corn
1 quart chicken stock, or water
1 tablespoon rice wine, optional
1 teaspoon salt, or to taste
1/4 teaspoon ground pepper, or to taste
1/2 cup minced ham
1/2 teaspoon minced fresh ginger, plus optional 1 teaspoon
2 ¹/₂ tablespoons cornstarch
3 tablespoons cold water
1 beaten egg

Bring the first 5 ingredients to a boil. Add the ham and 1/2 teaspoon ginger and again bring to a boil. Mix the cornstarch with the cold water until smooth. Add 3 tablespoons of the soup to the cornstarch mixture then very gradually add that mixture to the soup, stirring constantly to prevent lumps. Reduce heat and rapidly stir in the beaten egg. Serve immediately. Garnish with 1 teaspoon ginger if desired.
Makes 4 servings.

THREE-CUPS CHICKEN

Three-Cups Chicken is a traditional dish, using a cup of rice wine, a cup of soy sauce, and a cup of sesame oil. However, the cup is a *bei-zi*, which actually equals 1/2 cup measurement. This basic blend may be used to season or marinate numerous Asian dishes. For this recipe, the mixture may be varied slightly for a sweeter flavor.

Basil or *chiu-tseng-ta* is a popular seasoning in Taiwan because of its aroma and sweet, mild taste. To use fresh basil, pull the leaves from the stems and wash thoroughly. Although this recipe calls for whole leaves, the leaves may be shredded or chopped. If fresh basil is not available, use 1/3 the amount of dry basil, or about 2 to 3 teaspoons for Three-Cups Chicken.

9 cloves garlic, peeled and sliced
1 to 2 minced chili peppers
2 tablespoons minced fresh ginger
1 cut-up chicken (about 1 1/2 to 2 pounds),
  OR 4 chicken breasts, cut into bite-sized pieces
1/2 cup sesame oil
1/2 cup soy sauce
1/2 cup rice wine,
  OR 1/4 cup each rice wine and Shaohsing wine (available at Oriental markets)
1 teaspoon raw or white sugar
1/4 teaspoon ground white pepper, or to taste
1/4 cup fresh basil leaves

Place all the ingredients except the basil leaves in a deep wok. Bring to a boil, then lower the heat and simmer for 30 to 35 minutes. Remove the chicken to a heated platter. Stir-fry the basil leaves in the juices. Garnish the chicken with the basil. Drizzle 2 tablespoons sauce over the chicken, and serve the remaining sauce in a dish for dipping.
Makes 4 servings.

SQUASH STIR-FRIED WITH RICE NOODLES

2 green onions, minced
1 tablespoon dried shrimp flakes, optional
1 tablespoon sesame oil
1/2 teaspoon salt, or to taste
1 teaspoon raw or white sugar, or to taste
1/4 teaspoon white pepper, or to taste
1 pound pumpkin or Hubbard squash, peeled and finely chopped
1 cup chicken broth
1 can (61/2 ounces) clams
1 package (14 ounces) rice noodles, cooked
2 green onions, finely sliced
1 chili pepper, minced, optional

Stir-fry the minced green onions and shrimp flakes in the oil for 1 minute.
Add the salt, sugar, pepper, squash, and broth to the mixture and cook over a
low to medium flame until the squash is tender, about 10 minutes. Add more
broth if necessary. When the squash is tender, add the clams and heat through.
To this mixture, add the cooked rice noodles. Stir constantly to blend the
ingredients and heat through. Garnish with the finely sliced green onions and,
if desired, minced chili pepper.
Serves 4.

BEAN SPROUTS WITH MUSTARD GREENS AND CILANTRO

Cilantro is also known as Chinese parsley. It adds a robust flavor reminiscent of sage and citrus. To use, rinse well and gently remove the tender leaves from the stems. Use the leaves whole or chopped, depending upon the recipe.

1 cup sliced shiitake mushrooms
3 cups mung bean sprouts
2 cups coarsely chopped mustard greens
1/4 cup plus 3 tablespoons chopped cilantro
1/4 cup sesame oil
2 tablespoons soy sauce, or to taste
1/2 teaspoon cornstarch

Rinse the vegetables and pat dry. Stir-fry the vegetables and 1/4 cup cilantro in the sesame oil quickly at a high temperature, stirring the vegetables constantly to prevent burning. Combine the soy sauce and cornstarch, adding a little water if necessary, to form a thin paste. Whisk the mixture into the vegetables, making sure to coat them evenly. Serve immediately, garnishing with 3 tablespoons cilantro, if desired.

Serves 4.

MONGOLIAN FIRE POT
for Four

Mongolian Fire Pot
Transparent Bean Noodles
Chili Hunan Sauce
Black Bean Sauce
Sliced Oranges and Apples
Candied Ginger

Nothing creates a cozier feeling on a cold winter night than huddling around a Mongolian Fire Pot! Even better, it's the easiest Chinese meal to make—almost no preparation or clean up. Using chopsticks or long fondue forks, everyone cooks their own meat, vegetables, or shellfish in the bubbling broth. It is the forerunner of the one-dish meal.

Traditionally, a Mongolian fire pot is used for cooking. Small slivers of charred wood fuel the flame in the central cylinder, while sparks shoot out the top of the fire pot. A modern-day counterpart (and safer method) is the electric fondue pot.

Seat everyone around the fire pot or fondue pot. Surround the vessel with platters of sliced meat, vegetables, shellfish, and sauces. Arrange chopsticks or long fondue forks at each place setting, so the members can cook their own dinner, piece by piece. Spoon the sauces onto each plate, so everyone can dip the tidbits. It's a fun way to spend an informal evening, talking and laughing. All you have to do is keep the broth bubbling! The rest takes care of itself.

MONGOLIAN FIRE POT

Traditionally the meat is sliced while frozen, the result being *very* thin circles of meat, which are rolled into easily managed pieces for skewering and cooking.

2 quarts vegetable or beef broth
1/2 pound very thinly sliced beef or lamb
1 pound cleaned and shelled shrimp or sea scallops
1 small head (about 1 pound) cabbage, broken into leaves
2 cups mung bean sprouts
2 cups straw mushrooms (available at Oriental markets),
  OR 2 cups sliced button mushrooms
8 baby bok choy, optional (available at Oriental markets)
2 cups cooked, transparent bean noodles (available at Oriental markets),
  OR 2 cups cooked rice noodles

Heat the broth in a 3-quart pot. Carefully transfer the hot broth to the fire pot or fondue pot, or bring the broth to a boil in the fire pot or fondue pot. (Exercise caution—remember this is *hot!*) Using chopsticks or long forks, fondue style, dip a piece of meat or vegetable in the boiling broth until it is cooked. Next dip it in sauce (recipes below). When it has cooled, eat. It's as simple as that!

CHILI HUNAN SAUCE

1/2 tablespoon minced green onion
1/2 tablespoon minced fresh ginger
1/2 tablespoon minced garlic
1/2 teaspoon crushed chili pepper, or to taste
1 tablespoon sesame oil
1/4 cup soy sauce
1/4 cup water
3 tablespoons rice or wine vinegar
3 tablespoons raw or refined sugar
1 teaspoon cornstarch, or to taste
1/4 teaspoon ground white pepper, or to taste
2 tablespoons finely sliced green onion

Stir-fry the onion, ginger, garlic, and chili pepper in the oil until wilted, about 1 minute. Except for the finely sliced green onion, mix the remaining ingredients, making sure to dissolve the cornstarch. Whisk the liquid mixture into the spices and stir constantly over a low flame until the sauce is smooth and slightly thickened. (It should have a thin consistency.) Garnish with the sliced green onion.

Makes 1 cup sauce.

BLACK BEAN SAUCE

2 tablespoons minced fermented black beans (available at Oriental markets)
1/2 tablespoon minced chives
1/2 tablespoon minced fresh ginger
1/2 tablespoon minced garlic
1 tablespoon sesame oil
1 tablespoon shrimp oil, optional (available at Oriental markets)
1/4 cup soy sauce
1/4 cup water
3 tablespoons Shaohsing wine (available at Oriental markets)
3 tablespoons raw or white sugar
1 teaspoon cornstarch, or to taste
1/4 teaspoon ground white pepper, or to taste
2 tablespoons chopped fresh cilantro

Stir-fry the fermented black beans, chives, ginger, and garlic in the oil for 1 minute. Except for the cilantro, mix the remaining ingredients, making sure to dissolve the cornstarch. Whisk the liquid mixture into the spices and stir constantly over a low flame until the sauce is smooth and slightly thickened. (It should have a thin consistency.) Garnish with the cilantro.

Makes 1 cup sauce.

SEAFOOD PARTY BUFFET
for 10 to 12

Abalone and Vegetable Ball Soup
Piquant Wontons
Clams with Black Bean Sauce
Sole Roll-Ups in Ginger Crab Sauce
Stir-Fried Shrimp with Broccoli
Sea Scallops Tossed with Noodles
Star Fruit and Kiwi Slices
Fresh Strawberries
Assorted Cakes

Seafood is so plentiful in Taiwan that some of its residents have become spoiled. Fishermen from seaside towns cast their nets not once, but twice a day, allowing customers to purchase fresh fish in the morning and again after noon. Although this may not be practical for most of us, be meticulous about selecting only the freshest seafood possible. Spices, seasonings, or vegetables are secondary to the success of shellfish recipes. Fresh seafood is the key!

ABALONE AND VEGETABLE BALL SOUP

When serving soup at a buffet, present it in a rice cooker. Set the temperature to warm, keep a ladle and cups nearby, and let guests help themselves.

3 large carrots (about 1 pound)
1 turnip (about 1 pound)
1 cucumber (about 1 pound)
6 cups vegetable broth
1 teaspoon salt, or to taste
1/2 teaspoon ground white pepper, or to taste
1 teaspoon rice wine (available at Oriental markets)
1 can (15 ounces) abalone
2 tablespoons thinly sliced green onion

Peel the carrots, turnip, and cucumber. Using a melon baller, scoop balls from the vegetables and combine with all the ingredients except the abalone and green onion in a 3-quart saucepan. Bring to a boil, then lower heat and simmer for 10 minutes, or until the vegetables are tender. Slice the abalone into very thin strips. Add the abalone and its juice to the soup. Heat for 5 minutes, or until the abalone is tender and heated through. Garnish with a sprinkling of green onions.
Makes 8 to 10 cups soup.

PIQUANT WONTONS

1 pound shelled shrimp
1/2 pound mushrooms
1/4 pound fresh spinach
1 ¹/₂ tablespoons soy sauce, or to taste
1 tablespoon Shaohsing wine (available at Oriental markets)
1/4 teaspoon ground white pepper, or to taste
1 pound (about 48) wonton wrappers (recipe follows)
1 can (6 ounces) pineapple juice
1/2 cup rice or white vinegar
1/2 cup raw or white sugar
2 tablespoons cornstarch
1 tablespoon water
1/2 cup coarsely chopped Chinese Refrigerated Pickles (see recipe page 97)
1 cup sesame oil

Remove the veins from the shrimp. Mince the shrimp, mushrooms, and spinach by hand or using a food processor. Combine the mixture with 1/2 tablespoon of the soy sauce, Shaohsing wine, and pepper. Place 1 teaspoon mixture into the center of each wonton. Gather the edges and pinch together, creating a small, rounded pouch. Keep the filled wontons under a damp towel or plastic wrap to prevent them from drying out.

Blend the juice, vinegar, and sugar in a saucepan, and bring to a boil. Mix the cornstarch with 1 tablespoon soy sauce and the water. Whisk that into the pineapple liquid and simmer, stirring occasionally, for 2 to 3 minutes, or until thickened. Fold in the pickles and allow sauce to simmer over very low heat.

Heat the oil in a wok. Working with 10 to 12 wontons at a time, deep-fry them for 3 minutes, or until the outsides are golden brown, and the shrimp is thoroughly cooked. Drain on absorbent towels. To serve, spoon hot pineapple sauce over all.

Makes 48 wontons.

WONTON WRAPPERS

4 cups sifted, all-purpose flour
1 teaspoon salt
2 eggs, beaten
1 cup cold water

Mix the flour and salt. Form a well in the center for the eggs and water.
Combine the ingredients, shaping into a soft ball. Knead the dough for 4 to 5
minutes, or until smooth and elastic. Divide into 4 parts. Roll 1 ball at a time
into a 14-inch square about 1/16 inch thick. Use a 3-inch cookie cutter or a
glass rim to cut the dough into rounds. (For soup or deep-fried wontons, cut
into 3 $^1/_2$-inch squares.) Cover the completed wontons with a damp towel
while working with the other 3 dough balls. These may be made ahead,
wrapped in foil, and frozen.
Makes 48 wrappers.

CLAMS WITH BLACK BEAN SAUCE

4 dozen fresh clams
1/2 cup fermented, salted black beans
2 tablespoons minced fresh ginger
4 cloves garlic, minced
1/2 cup thinly sliced green onion
1/2 cup sesame oil
2 cups vegetable or chicken broth
1 tablespoon soy sauce, or to taste
2 tablespoons rice wine
5 cups hot, cooked noodles
1 cup chopped cilantro

Scrub clams under running water and set aside. Discard any clams that do not shut when tapped. Combine the beans, ginger, garlic, onions, and oil in a wok. Stir-fry for 3 minutes.

Add the broth, soy sauce, and rice wine and bring to a rolling boil. Carefully add the clams. When the mixture again comes to a boil, lower the heat, cover, and simmer for 8 to 10 minutes, or until the clamshells open. Discard any clams that do not open.

Arrange the hot noodles in a deep serving bowl. Spoon the clams and sauce over the noodles. Garnish liberally with cilantro. Keep a rice bowl of cilantro nearby for guests to add more cilantro.
Makes 10 to 12 servings.

SOLE ROLL-UPS IN GINGER CRAB SAUCE

Ginger, also known as ginger root, is a gnarled root with a brown outer skin that must be peeled or scraped off before using. Its refreshingly pungent flavor and aroma make it a staple ingredient in many Chinese dishes. Ginger is sold fresh or in jars or cans. Fresh ginger will keep for several weeks if wrapped in plastic and refrigerated.

2 pounds fillet of sole
1/4 cup finely chopped green onion
1/4 cup plus 2 tablespoons rice wine
1/4 cup plus 2 tablespoons sesame oil
1 tablespoon minced fresh ginger
1 teaspoon salt, or to taste
1/4 teaspoon ground white pepper
3 tablespoons cornstarch
1/2 cup water
1 cup flaked fresh crabmeat
2 1/2 cups chicken broth
1/2 cup milk
3 green onions, cut into 1 1/2-inch slivers
1 piece (about 2 inches) pared ginger, cut into 1 1/2-inch slivers

Trim each fillet to be about 6 inches long and 1/4 inch thick. Combine the finely chopped green onion, 2 tablespoons of the wine, 2 tablespoons of the oil, minced ginger, salt, and pepper. Coat each fillet in the mixture. Marinate for 30 minutes. Roll up each fillet, jellyroll style. Tucking the open ends underneath, arrange the fillets in a heatproof dish. Secure the dish on a steamer rack. Cover and steam over boiling water for 10 to 12 minutes, or until the fillets are opaque and easily flaked with a fork. Transfer the fillets to a serving platter and keep warm.

Combine the cornstarch, water, and 1/4 cup wine. Heat 1/4 cup oil in a wok. Add the crabmeat and stir-fry for 2 minutes. Blend in the cornstarch mixture, broth, and milk. Simmer, stirring, for 3 minutes, or until the sauce begins to thicken. Ladle the crab sauce over the fillets. Garnish with the slivered green onions and slivered ginger.
Serves 10 to 12.

STIR-FRIED SHRIMP WITH BROCCOLI

Peanut oil is lighter in both color and flavor than sesame oil. Made from pressed peanuts, this oil has a high smoking point. (It only begins to smoke at very high temperatures.) In comparison, sesame oil begins to smoke at a much lower temperature than peanut oil.

2 pounds shelled, deveined shrimp
1/4 cup peanut or vegetable oil
1 pound mushrooms, sliced
1 pound fresh broccoli, cut in bite-sized pieces
1 cup chicken broth
1 tablespoon cornstarch
1/2 teaspoon salt, or to taste
1/4 teaspoon ground white pepper, or to taste
1 teaspoon raw or white sugar
Parsley sprigs

Stir-fry the shrimp and oil in a wok over high heat for 3 to 4 minutes, or until the shrimp begin to turn pink. Add the mushrooms and broccoli and stir-fry for 2 to 3 minutes, or until the vegetables are tender-crisp. Blend the remaining ingredients except the parsley. Stir into the shrimp mixture and stir-fry over low heat for 2 to 3 minutes, or until the sauce thickens. Remove to a heated platter and garnish with parsley sprigs.
Serves 10 to 12.

SEA SCALLOPS TOSSED WITH NOODLES

Chinese-style egg noodles may be purchased fresh, frozen, or dried. They may be boiled, stir-fried, deep-fried, or braised; the cooking time and method vary with the type of noodle.

24 ounces Chinese egg noodles
3/4 cup sesame oil
1/2 cup oyster sauce (available at Oriental markets or see page 82)
1/2 cup soy sauce, or to taste
1 tablespoon raw or white sugar
1/2 teaspoon ground white pepper, or to taste
1 tablespoon minced ginger
2 cloves garlic, minced
1 pound fresh sea scallops, quartered
1 pound mung bean sprouts
1/2 cup chives, sliced in 1-inch lengths

Prepare noodles according to directions on package. Drain thoroughly and mix well with 1/4 cup of sesame oil. Set aside and keep warm. Mix the oyster sauce, soy sauce, sugar, and pepper. Stir into the noodles and toss to coat.

Combine 1/2 cup of sesame oil, the ginger, and garlic in a wok. Stir-fry for 1 minute. Add the scallops. Stir-fry for 1 to 2 minutes, or until the scallops become opaque. Add the sprouts and chives. Stir-fry for 1 minute, or until the vegetables begin to wilt. Add the noodles to the scallop mixture and heat thoroughly over a low flame. Serve on 1 or 2 large platters.
Makes 8 to 10 servings.

Spring:
DRAGON BOAT FESTIVAL

The Dragon Boat Festival, also called Double Five because it occurs on the fifth day of the fifth month of the Lunar Calendar, is one of the three most important Chinese festivals, Lunar New Year and Mid-Autumn Moon Festival being the other two.

The festival commemorates a statesman known as Chu Yuan, who served the Chinese emperor 2300 years ago. Wrongfully discredited by his rivals, Chu Yuan drowned himself to escape disfavor with the emperor. Dreading the death of an honest politician, the townspeople raced to rescue him by boat. Every year since then, teams of rowers have reenacted the deed by racing in boats that are painted to resemble dragons.

The traditional food for Dragon Boat Festival is *Tzungtzu* or Bamboo Rice Dumplings, which are triangularly shaped dumplings wrapped in bamboo leaves and then steamed. The "salty" variety contains bits of meat, shrimp, eggs, or peanuts and is eaten as an entrée. The "sweet" variety is made with sticky white rice, filled with a sweet red bean mixture, and eaten for dessert. Find both varieties of Bamboo Rice Dumplings in Oriental markets.

DRAGON BOAT FESTIVAL
Dinner

Hot & Sour Egg Drop Soup
Bamboo Rice Dumplings (Tzungtzu)
Stir-Fried Bean Sprouts with Red and Green Peppers
Stir-Fried Bamboo Shoots with Scallions and Garlic
Red-Bean Dumplings
Fresh Longans and Loquats

HOT & SOUR EGG DROP SOUP

Tofu, also known as bean curd, is available in many forms: fresh, canned, frozen, prepackaged, dried, and prepared. An inexpensive source of protein, it is made from pureed soybeans, pressed into a custard texture, similar to that of a soft cheese. Nearly tasteless on its own, it absorbs the flavor of its surrounding ingredients, making tofu a truly blank canvas in the culinary arts.

1/2 cup julienned pork
1 teaspoon plus 3 tablespoons cornstarch
2 tablespoons sesame oil
1 tablespoon soy sauce, or to taste
6 cups (1 1/2 quarts) chicken or vegetable broth
1/2 cup straw mushrooms
1/2 cup sliced button mushrooms
1/2 cup julienned carrot
1 cup firm tofu, cut into matchstick-sized slices
1/4 cup water
2 tablespoons rice or white vinegar
1 teaspoon salt, or to taste
1/2 teaspoon white pepper, or to taste
2 eggs, beaten

Dredge the pork in 1 teaspoon of the cornstarch. Then brown it in the sesame oil and soy sauce. Add the broth, bring to a boil, and cook for 5 minutes. Add the mushrooms and carrot and simmer over low flame for 15 minutes, or until the vegetables are tender, and the pork is thoroughly cooked. Add the tofu. Simmer until heated through. Combine 3 tablespoons cornstarch, the water, vinegar, salt, and pepper. Whisk until smooth. Then gradually add the cornstarch mixture into the hot soup, stirring to avoid lumps. When the soup is thickened, rapidly stir in the beaten eggs until the eggs strands float.
Makes 4 to 6 servings.

STIR-FRIED BEAN SPROUTS
WITH RED AND GREEN PEPPERS

Mung bean sprouts are the pale shoots of the plant, available fresh or canned. Use fresh if possible. Otherwise, rinse the canned sprouts under running water. Keep fresh or open cans of sprouts covered with water in the refrigerator until ready to use.

1 large green pepper, thinly sliced
1 quart boiling water
4 cups fresh mung bean sprouts
1 chili pepper, minced
1/4 teaspoon salt, or to taste
1 tablespoon sesame oil, or to taste

Add the green pepper to the boiling water. Simmer for 2 to 3 minutes. Add the bean sprouts and blanch. Remove the vegetables with a slotted spoon and drain thoroughly. Add the vegetables to the remaining ingredients, stir-fry for 2 minutes, and serve immediately.
Makes 4 servings.

STIR-FRIED BAMBOO SHOOTS
WITH SCALLIONS AND GARLIC

Bamboo shoots are ivory-colored sprouts of the tropical bamboo. Tender-crisp, they add texture and a mildly sweet flavor to any meal.

2 cups (two 8-ounce cans) sliced bamboo shoots
1/2 cup finely chopped pork (leftovers work well)
1/4 cup sesame oil
6 green onions, cut into 3-inch lengths
1 clove garlic, minced
1 chili pepper, minced
1 tablespoon soy sauce

Rinse the bamboo shoots under running water. Stir-fry the shoots and pork in the oil over medium heat for 10 minutes, or until the bamboo is tender and the pork is thoroughly cooked. Add the remaining ingredients. Stir-fry all for 5 minutes, or until the green onions are tender.
Serves 4.

MONGOLIAN LAMB BARBECUE

Mongolian Lamb
Assorted Vegetables
Assorted Herbs and Seasonings
Assorted Condiments
Sesame Sauce
Spicy Hunan Sauce
Sweet and Sour Plum Sauce
Various Cakes
Fresh Lychees
Iced Tea with Lime Wedges

For a party with a new theme, have a Mongolian Barbecue! Everyone chooses their own vegetables, condiments, and sauces from a variety of offerings. Each serving is cooked individually in front of the guest. It's high drama even without the traditional drum stove. Try this for your next get-together. It will be an evening no one will forget!

Line up the guests cafeteria-style. Hand each a large bowl and chopsticks and let their imaginations be their guides.

Set out platters and bowls of various vegetables, condiments, and sauces, buffet-style, on a long table. At the end of the table, station a designated chef (or two, depending on the size of the crowd) to do the honors on an electric griddle or wok. Watch the fun begin!

MONGOLIAN LAMB

2 pounds boneless lamb leg or shoulder
1/2 cup sesame oil

Trim the meat and slice across the grain into very thin 2-inch-long slices.
Traditionally the meat is sliced while frozen, the result being very thin slivers
of meat that are easily managed pieces for barbecuing. Arrange slices on a
platter with a serving fork or tongs. Let guests help themselves.

Set out chilled bowls or platters of the following vegetables:
1 pound shredded zucchini
1/2 pound green pepper, thinly sliced
1/2 pound red bell pepper, thinly sliced
1/2 pound carrot, shredded
1 pound mung bean sprouts
1 head (2 pounds) napa cabbage
1 pound tomatoes, sliced
Tofu strips (a thoughtful alternative for vegetarians)

Set out chilled bowls of the following herbs and seasonings:
3 cups slivered green onion
2 cups coarsely chopped cilantro
2 cups coarsely chopped basil
1/2 cup minced fresh ginger
1/2 cup minced fresh garlic
1/2 cup thinly sliced chili peppers

Set out the following condiments, providing shakers, bottles, and ladles where
necessary:
Salt
Ground white pepper
Ground black pepper
Soy sauce
Rice wine vinegar
Sesame oil
Peanut oil
Vegetable oil

Invite the guests to experiment and try any combination of the above ingredients, filling their bowls as they progress toward the chef. The chef then dumps the bowl's ingredients onto the griddle or into the wok and stir-fries each serving of the meat, vegetables, and seasonings in 1 to 2 tablespoons oil for 3 to 4 minutes, or until the meat is thoroughly cooked and the vegetables are crisp-tender. The stir-fried meal is ladled onto a fresh plate, and the guest sits down to eat, while the next guest's meal is cooked.
Serves 10 to 12.

Provide the following dipping sauces near the place settings, for use after the food is cooked:

SESAME SAUCE

2 tablespoons sesame seeds
2 tablespoons soy sauce
2 tablespoons rice wine vinegar
2 tablespoons sesame oil
2 tablespoons thinly sliced green onion
1 tablespoon raw or brown sugar
1 clove garlic, minced

Heat the sesame seeds in a nonstick skillet, stirring constantly for 2 minutes, or until seeds begin to brown. Remove from heat, transfer to a small bowl, and combine with the remaining ingredients. Stir well and let flavors marry for 30 minutes before serving.
Makes 1 ¹/₂ cups sauce.

SPICY HUNAN SAUCE

1 tablespoon chili paste (available at Oriental markets)
1 tablespoon minced green onion
2 tablespoons sesame oil
1 tablespoon minced garlic
1 tablespoon minced ginger
2 tablespoons soy sauce
2 tablespoons water
2 tablespoons raw or brown sugar
1 tablespoon vinegar
1 teaspoon cornstarch
1/4 teaspoon ground white pepper

In a hot wok, stir-fry the chili paste, green onion, and sesame oil for 1 minute. Blend the remaining ingredients together in a cup, and stir into the onion mixture. Stir-fry over medium heat until the sauce begins to thicken. Serve at room temperature. Refrigerate any leftover sauce.
Makes 1 ¹/₂ cups.

SWEET AND SOUR PLUM SAUCE

1 teaspoon cornstarch
1/2 cup water
2 tablespoons sour plum jelly (available at Oriental markets)
2 tablespoons rock or white sugar
1 tablespoon ketchup
1 tablespoon wine vinegar

Mix the cornstarch in the water. Combine all the ingredients in a saucepan and heat for 5 to 6 minutes, or until the sugar has dissolved and the sauce begins to thicken. Serve at room temperature. Refrigerate any leftover sauce.
Makes 1 ¹/₄ cups sauce.

Taiwanese
WEDDING DINNER

Cold Cuts
Phoenix Claw Soup
Drunken Chicken
Buddha Jumps the Wall
Prawns in Rice Wine
Scallion Scallops with Mustard Greens
Stir-Fried Shrimp and Loofah
Pork Tenderloin Noodle Soup
Steamed Red Snapper
Dragon Eye Soup
Watermelon Ice
Papaya, Honeydew, and Guava Wedges

Taiwanese wedding dinners are rarely served in homes. Most often they are held in large restaurants or ballrooms, although occasionally they may be held outdoors under festive, temporary tents. Groups of 10 to 12 people share each table, and 8 to 10 tables of guests are not uncommon. In restaurants, the tables are round with revolving lazy Susans in the center. The hustling wait staff hurries platters and tureens of food to the lazy Susans, while the guests help themselves.

Food is served in a series of courses, 2 or 3 at a time, nonstop for an hour. Guests take only what they like, or they try a smidgeon of everything. Abundance and variety are the keys to a successful party. No one stops eating during the dinner hour; there is not enough time to finish the first courses before the next round of platters and tureens graces the tables, and before guests have had time to sample those, the platters are removed to make way for another, and yet another round of dishes. A successful wedding dinner leaves the guests groaning.

Wedding dinners always consist of even numbers of courses: 10, 12, or 14 although 12 is considered the ideal number. Even numbers convey the idea of harmony and constancy. In these twelve courses, the first consists of cold cuts. This is followed by soup, then an assortment of steamed meats, such as Buddha Jumps the Wall, chicken, vegetables, abalone, and another soup. Fish is always served as the last entrée for good luck. The final three courses consist of a sweet soup, dessert, and fresh fruit.

During the dinner, the bride and groom visit each table and offer the guests a toast. Rice wine and beer are plentiful, but tradition demands that guests never merely sip their drinks, but always raise their glasses in toasts, with both hands cupping their glasses, to their hosts or neighbors. Taiwanese weddings are very sociable affairs.

The bride truly is beautiful, having spent the entire day grooming for the event. A cosmetician applies her makeup. A hair stylist dresses her hair in an elaborate style, and she wears extravagant, rented gowns for the day. In the course of the wedding dinner, the bride changes gowns at least once and sometimes twice, sporting ornate ballroom gowns, period pieces, traditional Taiwanese wedding garb, or more recently white-lace western bridal gowns.

Enjoy the merriment of Taiwanese weddings right in your home. If not for a wedding, this could be an anniversary celebration. Experiment with several, or all, of the following dishes. And if you want to dress for the occasion, go ahead! It *is* the bride's day, even if it is the wedding day's tenth anniversary!

PHOENIX CLAW SOUP

Wood ears, also known as cloud ears or tree ears, is a type of dried mushroom that expands its size by 5 to 6 times when soaked in hot water. It has a subtle earthy flavor and a chewy texture. If using button mushrooms instead, no soaking is necessary.

Traditionally Phoenix Claw Soup is made from chicken feet. Yes, chicken claws are edible; in fact, they are considered a great delicacy in Taiwan. You have the option in this recipe of being bold and tasting chicken claws or opting for the more familiar chicken legs!

1/4 cup dried wood ears,
   OR 1 pound button mushrooms, sliced
2 cups hot water
18 chicken feet (available at Oriental markets),
   OR 10 chicken legs
1 pound white asparagus
10 thin slices fresh ginger
1 teaspoon salt, or to taste
3 quarts chicken broth
2 tablespoons sesame oil

Soak the dehydrated wood ears in the hot water for an hour. Drain, rinse, and slice into very thin strips. If using chicken claws, chop each into 3 pieces. Snap off and discard the tough bases of the asparagus and cut the spears widthwise into fourths.

Add all the ingredients except the asparagus to a 5-quart pot. Bring to a boil, then lower temperature and simmer for 15 minutes. If using chicken legs, remove the legs from the soup with tongs. When cool enough to handle, bone the meat and discard the bones. (Traditionally chicken skin is eaten with the meat. If preferred, discard the skin.) Return the chicken meat to the stockpot, along with the lower 3/4 of the asparagus stalks. Simmer for 3 to 4 minutes. Add the asparagus tips to the soup, and simmer for 2 to 3 minutes, or until the tips are tender. Serve immediately.
Serves 10 to 12.

DRUNKEN CHICKEN

2 broiler/fryer chickens, each about 3 pounds
12 green onions, trimmed and sliced
12 thin slices fresh ginger
3 stalks celery, sliced
1 quart chicken broth
4 cups Shaohsing wine
3 parsley sprigs

Chop the chickens into 8 parts each: 2 wings, 2 legs, 2 backs, and 2 breasts. Combine the chicken parts, green onions, ginger, celery, and broth in a 5-quart pot. Bring to a boil, lower heat, cover, and simmer for 30 to 35 minutes, or until the chickens are tender. Remove from heat. When chickens are cool enough to handle, cut into serving-sized pieces. To cut chickens Chinese-style, use a sharp cleaver, and chop each piece lengthwise into thirds. Chop the wings in half. Place pieces back into pot, add the wine, and marinate for 24 hours in the refrigerator. Serve cold on chilled platters, garnished with parsley sprigs. **Serves 10 to 12.**

BUDDHA JUMPS THE WALL

Buddha Jumps the Wall is a classic dish reserved for very special Taiwanese occasions. There is a good reason for this. Prepared in the traditional way, it requires intricate preparation for six consecutive days. Since most of us do not have the luxury of spending six days making one recipe for one meal, you will be happy to find a simplified version below. Buddha Jumps the Wall, also know as Buddha's Temptation, gets its name from the concept that even Buddha, the most devout vegetarian, would jump the wall of the monastery and renounce his vegan ways to taste this delicacy. Try it and judge for yourself!

1/4 cup dried wood ears
2 cups hot water
12 sea scallops
1/2 cup plus 2 tablespoons sesame oil
3 pounds stewing chicken, boned and cut-up
1 pound yams, peeled and cut-up
1 can (15 ounces) chopped abalone, drained
1 pound ham coarsely chopped
12 trimmed green onions, cut into 2-inch lengths
1/2 cup rice wine
1/2 cup raw or brown sugar
1/2 cup soy sauce, or to taste
1/2 teaspoon ground white pepper, or to taste
2 quarts chicken broth

Preheat the oven to 350°. Soak the dehydrated wood ears in the hot water for an hour. Drain, rinse, and slice into very thin strips. Stir-fry the scallops in 2 tablespoons of the oil in a hot wok for 3 to 4 minutes, or until just opaque. Remove the scallops and set aside. Stir-fry the chicken, several pieces at a time, in 1/2 cup of the oil, adding more oil as needed. Stir-fry each batch of chicken to a golden brown, about 4 to 5 minutes per batch. Combine all ingredients in an oven-roasting pan. Cover and bake, stirring every 30 minutes, for 3 1/2 hours, or until all the ingredients are tender. **Serves 10 to 12.**

PRAWNS IN RICE WINE

24 prawns
6 cups rice wine
12 slices fresh ginger
1/2 teaspoon salt
12 black peppercorns
1 dried plum, optional (available at Oriental markets)

Traditionally heads are left on prawns and are considered a delicacy. If you prefer, remove heads but leave the shells on the prawns. Bring the wine, ginger, salt, peppercorns, and plum to a boil in a 5-quart pot. Carefully add the prawns to the mixture. Bring again to a boil, then lower heat, and simmer for 3 to 4 minutes, or until the prawns become pink. Serve immediately.
Makes 12 servings.

SCALLION SCALLOPS WITH MUSTARD GREENS

1 pound sea scallops
14 scallions, trimmed and sliced
1 chili pepper, minced
6 tablespoons sesame oil
6 cups mustard greens
1 tablespoon rice wine (available at Oriental markets)
2 tablespoons raw or white sugar
1/2 teaspoon salt, or to taste
1/2 teaspoon ground white pepper, or to taste

Combine the scallops, 1/3 of the scallions, and all the chili with 3 tablespoons of the oil. Stir-fry for 4 to 5 minutes, or until the scallops become opaque. Remove the scallops to a heated platter. Add the mustard greens, 1/3 of the scallions, remaining 3 tablespoons oil, the wine, sugar, salt, and pepper. Stir-fry for 3 to 4 minutes, or until the mustard greens wilt. Add the scallops, and stir-fry until heated through. Arrange on a heated platter, and garnish with the remaining scallion rings.
Serves 10 to 12 as a side dish, or 4 as a main course.

STIR-FRIED SHRIMP AND LOOFAH

When young and tender, loofah is a delectable vegetable that resembles squash in both texture and taste. However, when dried, it is the same vegetable that is used as a bath sponge. When purchasing loofah, select firm, unblemished vegetables. The outer skin should have a dark green color, similar to that of a cucumber.

1 pound shrimp
6 green onions, trimmed and sliced
1 chili pepper, minced
1/2 cup sesame oil
2 pounds peeled loofah (available at Oriental markets)
2 celery stalks, julienned
1/2 teaspoon salt, or to taste
1/2 teaspoon ground white pepper, or to taste
1/2 cup vegetable or chicken broth
2 tablespoons fresh cilantro leaves

Remove the shells and veins from the shrimp. Rinse and pat dry. Combine the shrimp, onions, chili, and 1/4 cup of the oil in a hot wok. Stir-fry for 3 to 4 minutes, or until the shrimp turn pink. Remove shrimp and set aside.

Cut the loofah into 2 x 1/2-inch strips (4 cups). Add to the wok, along with the remaining 1/4 cup of oil, the celery, salt, and pepper. Stir-fry the ingredients for 3 to 4 minutes, or until the mixture begins to dry. Lower the heat, stir in the broth, and cover. Steam for 3 to 4 minutes, or until the loofah is tender and the liquid has been absorbed. Add the shrimp and stir-fry for 1 to 2 minutes, or until the shrimp are hot. Arrange on a heated serving platter, and garnish with the cilantro leaves.
Serves 10 to 12 as a side dish, or 4 as a main course.

PORK TENDERLOIN NOODLE SOUP

1 ¹/₂ pounds pork tenderloin, julienned
1 head (12 to 15 ounce) napa cabbage, shredded
5 tablespoons sesame oil
1/2 cup soy sauce, or to taste
1 tablespoon minced fresh ginger
3 quarts chicken broth
12 ounces thin Chinese egg noodles
24 green onions, sliced diagonally into 1-inch lengths

Combine the pork, cabbage, and oil in a wok. Stir-fry the ingredients for 6 to 8 minutes, or until the pork is thoroughly cooked and no longer pink. Add the soy sauce, ginger, and broth. Bring to a boil, reduce heat, cover, and simmer for 10 to 12 minutes. Carefully add the noodles and green onions. Again bring to a boil and simmer for 2 to 3 minutes, or until the noodles are tender. Serve immediately.
Serves 10 to 12.

STEAMED RED SNAPPER

Wedding feasts always serve fish as the final entrée. Fish are good-luck symbols in Taiwan. They indicate abundance and wealth. What better way to wish the newly wed couple happiness than by ending the meal with a sign that their lives will be filled with a surplus of love, money, and success?

2 (2 pounds each) whole red snappers
2 teaspoons salt, or to taste
1/4 cup ginger slivers, matchstick size
1/4 cup green onion slivers, matchstick size
1/2 cup sesame oil
1/2 cup soy sauce
12 kumquats, optional
8 cilantro sprigs

Clean and scale fish. Make 3 diagonal slits on each side of the fish. Rub the fish with salt.

Steam 1 fish at a time. Sprinkle 1 tablespoon each of ginger and onion on top of each fish. Place first fish in steamer, cover, and steam for 9 to 10 minutes per inch of thickness. When the first fish is cooked, remove it and keep warm while the second fish steams. Repeat for the second fish.

While the second fish steams, warm the sesame oil. Drizzle the soy sauce over the cooked fish. Sprinkle each with a tablespoon of ginger and green onions. Carefully drizzle the hot oil over the fish. Serve while still sizzling. Garnish with kumquats and cilantro sprigs.
Serves 10 to 12.

DRAGON EYE SOUP

Dragon Eye soup is a spring treat! Longan or *long-yan*, Chinese for dragon eye, is a sweet, seasonal fruit, similar to the lychee, with a rough outer skin and, when peeled, a soft round center like a huge grape—or dragon eye. It is harvested in May and early June, or you can purchase canned longan any time.

Taro is a root crop similar to sweet potatoes or yams, but it has a slightly lavender hue when boiled and a subtle flavor all of its own. Boxthorn fruit is a kind of berry that is used as both a spice and medicinal herb. Try all three exotic ingredients in this dessert soup for a refreshing conclusion to a balmy spring evening's meal.

1 pound taro (available at Oriental markets),
* OR 1 pound sweet potatoes, cooked and pared*
1 ¹/₂ quarts cold water, divided
2 cups hot water
1/2 cup boxthorn fruit (available at Oriental markets)
1/2 cup raw or white sugar
2 (20 ounce) cans longan in syrup (available at Oriental markets)
Pastilles (see recipe below)
1/2 cup salted, boiled peanuts,
* OR salted, roasted peanuts, optional*

Wash the taro (but do not pare) and cook in the cold water. Bring to a boil then lower heat and simmer for about 30 minutes, or until tender. When cool enough to handle, drain and peel.

Combine the cooked taro with the hot water, boxthorn fruit, and sugar in a 5-quart pan. Bring to a boil and then lower the heat. Fold in the longan with its juice. Heat through, but do not boil. Stir in the pastilles and peanuts. Serve immediately.
Serves 12.

PASTILLES

1 cup rice flour (available at Oriental markets)

Mix the flour and 1/4 cup water to form a stiff dough. Tear off one eighth to 1/4 teaspoonfuls dough, and roll between the palms of your hands to form small balls. When all the dough has been rolled into tiny balls, carefully drop them into boiling water. When the water comes to a boil, add a cup of cold water. Again bring to a boil. When the dough balls float to the surface of the boiling water, they are done. Remove with a slotted spoon and drain.
Makes 1 cup rice-flour pastilles.

WATERMELON ICE

1 large watermelon
1 ¹/₂ cups raw or white sugar
1 cup lime juice
12 fresh mint sprigs
12 thin lime rind twists

Blend watermelon chunks in a blender until liquefied. Strain and measure 12 cups of juice. Heat the watermelon juice, sugar, and lime juice in a 5-quart pan. Stirring occasionally, heat over medium flame for 12 to 15 minutes, or until the sugar is dissolved. Do not boil. When cool, transfer to shallow freezer trays, and place in freezer. Stirring mixture every 25 to 30 minutes to prevent solid ice crystals from forming, allow mixture to freeze into a very firm slush for 3 to 4 hours, or until it hardens to a sorbet consistency. Scoop into rice bowls to serve. Garnish each bowl with a fresh mint sprig and lime twist.
Serves 12.

Summer:
CHINESE VALENTINE'S DAY

Chinese Valentine's Day occurs on the seventh day of the seventh lunar month, usually in August. It's a celebration for yearning lovers, dating back to a legend about the Jade Emperor's seventh daughter, who was a seamstress. She fell in love with and married a cowherd who lived across the Milky Way, but when she neglected her sewing and weaving duties, the emperor ordered her home, allowing her to visit her husband only once a year. According to the myth, on the seventh day of the seventh month, crows fly in such a tight flight formation through the Milky Way, that the seamstress can walk across their wings to meet her husband.

Like the American version of Valentine's Day, lovers give each other small gifts and flowers, with cockcrow or *gi guang* (literally "king's crown") and gomphrena being the traditional flowers.

VALENTINE'S DAY DINNER
for Two

Oysters with Leeks
Piquant Lime Chicken in Swallow's Nest
Spicy Szechwan Eggplant
Date-Filled Wontons
Fresh Longans and Cherries

Prepare a love feast just for the two of you. Dim the lights. Create the mood as you set the table with your best china and linen. But don't use silverware. Use chopsticks—and feed each other. Decorate with fresh flowers and lacy paper lanterns. Prepare exotic recipes that traditionally have given rise to romantic ideas.

OYSTERS WITH LEEKS

1/2 pound shucked, fresh oysters
2 cloves garlic, minced
2 leeks, rinsed thoroughly and chopped into 1/2-inch slices
1/4 cup sesame oil
1 tablespoon soy sauce, or to taste
1/4 teaspoon ground white pepper
1 tablespoon chopped cilantro

Combine all ingredients except the cilantro in a hot wok. Stir-fry all for 4 to 5 minutes, or until the oysters are cooked and the leeks are tender. Garnish with the cilantro.
Serves 2.

The Best of Taiwanese Cuisine

PIQUANT LIME CHICKEN IN SWALLOW'S NEST

2 chicken breasts, boned and skinned
3 1/2 tablespoons cornstarch
1/4 teaspoon salt, or to taste
2 tablespoons water
2 egg yolks, beaten
1/4 cup sesame oil
2 green onions, sliced diagonally
1 cup chicken broth
1/4 cup freshly squeezed lime juice
3 tablespoons raw or dark brown sugar
2 tablespoons honey
1 teaspoon minced fresh ginger

Pound the chicken breasts with a mallet to flatten and tenderize. Combine 2 tablespoons of the cornstarch, the salt, water, and egg yolks in a shallow bowl. Heat the oil in a wok. Dip chicken into the cornstarch mixture, then stir-fry over high heat for 6 minutes, or until chicken is golden brown. Remove, drain on absorbent towels, and arrange each chicken breast in a Swallow's Nest (recipe follows). Garnish with the green onions.

Combine 1 1/2 tablespoons cornstarch and the remaining ingredients in the wok. Stirring constantly over low heat, cook the sauce for 3 to 4 minutes, or until it thickens. Spoon the sauce over the chicken breasts.
Serves 2.

SWALLOW'S NEST

These "nests" can be prepared up to three days in advance if wrapped in plastic and refrigerated, or, if frozen, they can be made up to three weeks in advance. Valentine's Day is a time for enjoying the fruits of your labor, not for laboring!

3 ounces Chinese egg noodles (about 2 cups cooked noodles)
Sesame oil for deep-frying

Prepare the noodles according to the directions on the package. Drain thoroughly on absorbent towels overnight, covered. Brush the inside of a medium strainer with oil. Spread half the noodles over it evenly. Brush the outside of a smaller strainer with oil. Press the second strainer against the noodles, sandwiching the noodles between the 2 strainers. Very carefully lower all into a wok half-filled with hot sesame oil. Deep-fry for 2 to 3 minutes, or until the first nest is golden brown. Remove from the oil and very carefully release the nest from the 2 strainers. Drain on absorbent towels. Repeat with the second nest. **Makes 2 nests.**

SPICY SZECHWAN EGGPLANT

1/2 pound Oriental eggplants (available at Oriental markets),
   OR 1 small domestic eggplant
2 green onions
1 teaspoon minced garlic
1 teaspoon minced fresh ginger
1 teaspoon black beans sauce
1/4 teaspoon sliced chili pepper, or to taste
2 tablespoons chicken broth
1 teaspoon soy sauce
1 teaspoon rice wine vinegar
1 teaspoon sugar
1/2 teaspoon Ten-Spice Powder (see recipe page 117)
3 tablespoons sesame oil
1 tablespoon water
1/2 teaspoon cornstarch

Slice unpeeled eggplant into 2 x 1/2-inch strips. Trim and finely slice the green onions. Reserve half for garnish. Combine half the onions with the garlic, ginger, black beans, and pepper; set aside. Blend the broth, soy sauce, vinegar, sugar, and ten-spice powder in a small bowl; set aside.

Heat 2 tablespoons of the oil in a wok. Stir-fry the eggplant over medium heat for 5 minutes, or until the eggplant is soft. Remove eggplant with a slotted spoon and set aside. Add the remaining 1 tablespoon oil and onion/garlic mixture to the wok. Stir-fry for 30 seconds. Fold in the eggplant and broth mixture. Bring to a boil and simmer, stirring occasionally, until the excess liquid has evaporated.

Whisk the water with the cornstarch. Stir into the eggplant and heat until sauce thickens. Remove to a serving platter. Garnish with the remaining green onions. **Serves 2.**

DATE-FILLED WONTONS

Use the peelings of only organically grown oranges.

4 (8-ounce) packages chopped, pitted dates
2 cups finely chopped walnuts
1/2 cup grated orange peel
1/2 cup orange juice, as needed
1 pound (3 ¹/₂-inch square) wontons, purchased or made (see recipe page 40)
3 cups peanut or vegetable oil
2 tablespoons confectioners' sugar

Combine the chopped dates, walnuts, and orange peel and roll into a large ball. If necessary, add a little orange juice to help make the mixture cohesive. Taking about 1 tablespoon of the mixture, roll it between your palms into a 1 x 1/3-inch cylinder. Place it in the center of a wonton and fold a wonton corner over it, tucking it beneath the date filling. Roll up, jellyroll fashion. Twist ends to secure. Add the oil to a wok or deep fryer and heat to 375°. Deep-fry 9 to 10 wontons at a time, turning occasionally, for 2 to 3 minutes, or until crisp and golden. Remove with a slotted spoon and drain on absorbent towels. Continue until all the wontons and filling are used. Dust with confectioners' sugar before serving. Make the day before, place in plastic bags or airtight containers, and refrigerate. Pop a few into the microwave to reheat for the two of you, and enjoy.
Makes 48 wontons.

HUNGRY GHOST
Menu

Wonton Soup
Fresh Lotus Root Salad
Baked Pork Ribs Rubbed with Mustard Celery Seed
Straw Mushrooms and Snow Peas
Orange and Honeydew Wedges
Candied Lotus Seeds
Grape Tomatoes*

Taiwan has a counterpart to Halloween, but, instead of one day, this celebration lasts a month. The seventh lunar month is known as *Hungry Ghost Month*. The first day is called the *Opening of the Gates of Hades*; the last is called the *Closing of the Gates of Hades*. People believe that for a month, hungry ghosts walk the streets, looking for a good party. The fifteenth day of the seventh month is especially ominous. Many Taiwanese stay home that day, hoping to avoid an unlucky encounter with a ghost out enjoying the festivities. They display fruit, alcohol, and cigarette offerings on small tables outside their front doors. They light incense and burn ghost money (silver paper rectangles that look like money) to appease the hungry ghosts. They hold colorful parades, wear over-sized effigies of Buddhist saints, and light millions of firecrackers, hoping to frighten away the evil spirits. What better time to hold a party?

*Grape tomatoes are very sweet tomatoes about the size of grapes. These are considered a fruit, not a vegetable, and are eaten for dessert.

WONTON SOUP

1/2 pound lean pork, chopped
1 tablespoon soy sauce, or to taste
1 teaspoon minced fresh ginger
1/2 teaspoon salt, or to taste
6 tablespoons (10 ounces) frozen spinach, chopped and drained
1/2 pound (3 1/2-inch square) wonton wrappers, purchased or made
  (see recipe page 40)
2 quarts boiling water
6 cups chicken broth
1 cup coarsely chopped fresh spinach leaves

Combine the pork, soy sauce, ginger, and salt in a large bowl. Fold in the cooked and drained spinach and mix well.

Place a teaspoon of the filling just below the center of each wrapper. Fold o end of the wonton over, tucking it beneath the filling. Dampen the edge to secure it. Roll it between your hands to form a small cylinder. Pull the 2 en down beneath the roll until they overlap. Using damp fingers, pinch the en firmly to secure.

Drop the wontons into rapidly boiling water. Bring again to a boil, then low heat and simmer for 5 to 6 minutes, or until pork is thoroughly cooked, yet wontons are still a bit firm. Drain the wontons and discard the water. Add broth to the 5-quart pot and bring to a boil. Add the fresh spinach and wo tons. Bring to a boil once more then serve immediately.
Serves 4 to 6.

FRESH LOTUS ROOT SALAD

1 pound fresh lotus root (available at Oriental markets)
1 tablespoon soy sauce
1 tablespoon rice wine vinegar
2 tablespoons raw or white sugar
1 tablespoon sesame oil
1/4 teaspoon salt, or to taste

Rinse the lotus root under running water, peel, and discard both ends. Slice root into 1/8-inch-thick slices and place slices in water to prevent discoloration until root is completely sliced. Drain the lotus root then blanch in boiling water for 5 to 6 minutes. Drain, rinse with cold water, and pat dry with absorbent towels.

Combine the remaining ingredients. Spoon the dressing over the lotus root slices and stir to coat evenly. Marinate in the refrigerator for an hour, stirring occasionally. Arrange slices in a circular pattern on a serving platter.
Serves 4 to 6.

BAKED PORK RIBS RUBBED
WITH MUSTARD CELERY SEED

4 tablespoons cornstarch
2 tablespoons Mustard Celery Seed Rub (recipe follows)
2 pounds pork back ribs, cut into bite-sized pieces
1/4 cup sesame oil
2 tablespoons sliced chili pepper
3 tablespoons soy sauce
1 tablespoon raw or white sugar
2 tablespoons Ginger Vinegar (recipe follows)
1/2 cup water

Preheat oven at 350°. Combine the cornstarch and Mustard Celery Seed Rub in a cellophane cooking pouch. Add the ribs and shake to coat evenly. Stir-fry the ribs with the oil in a wok for 3 to 4 minutes, or until lightly browned. Add the chili pepper, soy sauce, sugar, Ginger Vinegar, and water. Stir-fry over low heat until the sauce begins to thicken.

Transfer the ribs and sauce to a baking dish and bake for 35 to 40 minutes, or until the ribs are tender and richly glazed.
Makes 4 to 6 servings.

MUSTARD CELERY SEED RUB

1/2 teaspoon dry mustard powder
1/2 teaspoon celery seed
1 teaspoon salt
1 tablespoon paprika
1/2 cup raw or dark brown sugar

Combine ingredients and store in an airtight container away from the sunlight. Before baking or grilling cuts of pork or beef, rub the mixture onto meat to enhance its flavor.
Makes 2/3 cup spice rub.

GINGER VINEGAR

2 tablespoons finely minced fresh ginger
1 tablespoon rice wine
1 cup white wine vinegar

Combine the ingredients in a clean jar. Cover tightly with lid and refrigerate for 2 days. Strain the mixture through a fine sieve. Strain it again through a coffee filter. Pour into a clean, airtight bottle. If refrigerated, the flavored vinegar will keep for a week. Use in any recipe that requires vinegar and ginger. **Makes 1 cup.**

STRAW MUSHROOMS AND SNOW PEAS

Snow peas, also know as pea pods or Chinese peas, are flat green pods that are collected before the peas have fully matured. There is no need to shell these immature peas. Only trim off the ends and the stringy substance along the tops. Snow peas add bright green color, a crunchy texture, and a delicate flavor to any Chinese dish.

1 pound fresh snow peas
1/4 cup peanut or vegetable oil
1/2 teaspoon salt, or to taste
1 pound straw mushrooms, rinsed and drained
1/2 cup water
1/4 cup oyster sauce (prepared or see recipe page 82)
1 tablespoon soy sauce
1/8 teaspoon ground white pepper, or to taste
1 teaspoon raw or white sugar

Remove the ends and strings from the snow peas. Add the snow peas, oil, and salt to a wok. Stir-fry the mixture for 3 to 5 minutes, or until the peas are tender-crisp. Add the remaining ingredients. Stir-fry for 1 to 2 minutes, or until mushrooms and peas are tender. Serve immediately.
Makes 4 to 6 servings.

BA-BA'S DAY
(Father's Day)

Father's Day in Taiwan comes in August, not June. It's known as *Ba-ba* Day or Double-Eight because it falls on the eighth day of the eighth month. The Mandarin Chinese word for eight is *ba*, so the eighth day of the eighth month is *ba-ba*. *Ba-ba* also happens to be the Mandarin word for papa or father, so it's a natural progression for that date to be Father's Day in Taiwan.

Ba-ba's Day Dinner

Chicken Soup with Shiitake Mushrooms and Carrots
Five-Colored Pork and Shrimp Rolls
Steamed Asparagus with Garlic Sesame Sauce
Wilted Chinese Broccoli with Oyster Sauce
Zucchini and Loofah
Stir-Fried Crab with Bamboo Shoots
Watermelon Slices
Jellied Cocoa Pudding

The Best of Taiwanese Cuisine

CHICKEN SOUP WITH
SHIITAKE MUSHROOMS AND CARROTS

1/2 cup finely sliced chicken
1 teaspoon salt, or to taste
1/4 teaspoon ground white pepper, or to taste
1 tablespoon cornstarch
1 tablespoon rice wine (available at Oriental markets)
2 tablespoons sesame oil
4 cups chicken broth
1/2 cup sliced shiitake mushrooms
1/2 cup thinly sliced carrots

Dredge the sliced chicken in the salt, pepper, and cornstarch. Stir-fry in a wok with the rice wine and sesame oil for 2 to 3 minutes. Add the chicken broth, mushrooms, and carrots, and simmer, covered, for 15 minutes, or until chicken is cooked and vegetables are tender.
Serves 4.

FIVE-COLORED PORK AND SHRIMP ROLLS

To-gan is a dried variety of tofu that has been steeped in various spices and seasonings. Having absorbed those flavors, to-gan then imparts them to any dish to which it is added.

1/2 pound pork tenderloin, thinly sliced
12 freshwater shrimp
1 quart salted, boiling water
2 tablespoons raw or light brown sugar
2 tablespoons soy sauce
2 cups mung bean sprouts
1 large cucumber
1/2 teaspoon salt, or to taste
1/2 pound dried tofu (to-gan)
1/2 teaspoon sesame oil
10 (3-inch round) wonton wrappers (see recipe page 40)
2 tablespoons chopped fresh parsley
2 tablespoons peanut powder (available at Oriental markets), or peanut butter
Fresh parsley sprigs
3 green tomatoes, sliced

Bring the pork tenderloin and shrimp to a gentle boil in the salted water. Cook for 6 minutes or until the pork and shrimp are done. Remove from the water with a slotted spoon. When the pork and shrimp are cool enough to handle, finely chop the pork tenderloin and shell the shrimp. Mix with the sugar and soy sauce.

Blanch the bean sprouts in the boiling water. Remove and drain thoroughly. Slice the cucumber into pencil-sized strips. Salt and allow strips to drain for 5 minutes on paper towels. Slice the dried tofu into pencil-sized strips.

Oil the wonton wrappers sparingly. Working with one wrapper at a time, place it on a plate. Spread one-tenth each of the pork, shrimp, and bean sprouts on the wrapper. Add a cucumber slice, 2 tofu strips (arranged lengthwise), chopped parsley, and peanut powder. Roll tightly, slightly dampening the wonton ends to adhere. Slice in half width-wise. Arrange on a platter and garnish with fresh parsley sprigs and tomato slices. Continue until all the ingredients are used.
Serves 4.

STEAMED ASPARAGUS

Check asparagus carefully before purchasing. The tips should be compact, not flowery. The stalks should be firm, fresh, with a deep green color, not yellow or pale. The bottoms should be brittle, with an inch or two of woody base, which must be trimmed before cooking.

2 pounds fresh asparagus, or 6 to 8 stalks per person
Salted boiling water

Break off (do not cut) the woody base from each asparagus stalk. The woody base will snap off from the tender portion. Wash stalks thoroughly under running cold water.

Tie the stalks in serving-size bunches. Stand upright in a deep saucepan, which contains an inch of salted, boiling water. Cover and allow to steam for 15 minutes, or until the asparagus is tender but still crisp. Serve with Garlic Sesame Sauce (directions below).
Makes 4 servings.

GARLIC SESAME SAUCE

1 clove garlic, minced
1 ¹/₂ tablespoons sesame oil
2 tablespoons soy sauce
1 teaspoon sesame seeds

Stir-fry the garlic in the sesame oil for 1 minute. Whisk in the soy sauce. Remove from heat, and stir in the sesame seeds. Serve in a rice bowl as a dipping sauce or drizzle over the hot asparagus.
Makes 1/4 cup sauce.

WILTED CHINESE BROCCOLI WITH OYSTER SAUCE

Chinese Broccoli is not like common broccoli. Instead of the familiar bluish-green florets, it is the leaves of this delicate vegetable that are steamed or stir-fried and eaten.

1 pound fresh Chinese broccoli (available at Oriental markets)
1 quart salted, boiling water
2 tablespoons oyster sauce (see below)

Slice off the tough bottoms of the Chinese broccoli stalks. Discard any wilted leaves. Rinse thoroughly under cool running water and slice into 4-inch long pieces. Carefully add the broccoli to the boiling water and simmer for 2 minutes. Remove the broccoli carefully with a slotted spoon. Drain well. Top with oyster sauce and serve immediately.
Makes 4 servings.

OYSTER SAUCE

Commercial oyster sauce is a concentrated, brown sauce made of ground oysters, soy sauce, and brine. It is used as commonly in Taiwan as ketchup is in the United States. Also available in a vegetarian variety, oyster sauce enhances any dish, bringing out the various flavors of the other ingredients.

1 can (3 ³/₄ ounces) smoked oysters
1/2 cup rice wine
1/2 cup chicken broth
2 tablespoons soy sauce
1 tablespoon raw or brown sugar
1/2 teaspoon salt, or to taste
1/4 teaspoon ground white pepper, or to taste

Finely mince the oysters or, using a blender's pulse mode, pulverize the oysters in their liquid. Add all ingredients to a saucepan and simmer for 15 minutes. Strain, cool, cover, and refrigerate. Will keep up to a week in the refrigerator.
Makes 1 ¹/₂ cups sauce.

ZUCCHINI AND LOOFAH

When young and tender, loofah is a delectable vegetable that resembles squash in both texture and taste. However, when dried, it is the same vegetable that is used as a bath sponge. When purchasing loofah, select firm, unblemished vegetables. The outer skin should have a dark green color, similar to that of a cucumber.

1/2 pound zucchini
1/2 pound loofah (available at Oriental markets), or *summer squash*
2 tablespoons sesame oil
1 clove garlic, minced
1 tablespoon soy sauce, or to taste
1/4 cup water

Rinse the vegetables thoroughly. Score the zucchini with a fork and slice diagonally into 1/2-inch slices. Peel the loofah and cut diagonally into 1/2-inch slices. Combine with the oil and garlic and stir-fry over high heat for 1 to 2 minutes. Add the soy sauce and water. Cover and steam for 2 minutes, or until vegetable slices are tender but still crisp.
Makes 4 servings.

STIR-FRIED CRAB WITH BAMBOO SHOOTS

1/2 cup chopped pork
1/2 cup chopped mushrooms
1 cup (8-ounce can) thinly sliced bamboo shoots
2 green onions, sliced
1 clove garlic, minced
1/4 cup sesame oil
1 cup fish or vegetable stock
1/4 teaspoon cornstarch
1 teaspoon water
1 cup crabmeat, cooked
2 tablespoons oyster sauce (available at Oriental markets or see page 82)
3 egg whites, stiffly beaten

Preheat the oven to 475°. Stir-fry the pork, mushrooms, bamboo shoots, green onions, and garlic in the oil for 6 minutes, or until the pork is thoroughly cooked and the vegetables are tender. Add the stock to the vegetables. Combine the cornstarch and water and stir into the mixture. Allow it to come to a boil then lower heat and simmer for 5 minutes, stirring occasionally. Carefully pick over the crabmeat, discarding any bits of shell. Add the crabmeat and oyster sauce and heat through. Pour the mixture into a large serving bowl. Mound the egg whites in the center, spooning several tablespoons of the sauce over all. Place in the oven for 3 to 4 minutes, or until the egg whites are golden brown.
Serves 4.

JELLIED COCOA PUDDING

Many Taiwanese meals conclude with a thin custard or jelly, as it is called. The texture is very light, and the taste is pleasing, not heavy or overly sweet. Jellied Cocoa Pudding is especially cool and refreshing on a hot August night!

4 candied cherries
1 can (15 ounces) sliced peaches
1 cup shelled raw peanuts
1 cup shelled raw almonds
6 tablespoons cornstarch
2/3 cup raw or white sugar
1 tablespoon cocoa powder

Place a candied cherry in each of 4 teacups. Top each cherry with a cut-up peach slice. Process the peanuts, almonds, and 3 cups water in a blender until liquefied. Strain the juice, discarding the pulp. Combine the cornstarch with 6 tablespoons water. Heat the juice, sugar, and cornstarch mixture over high heat, stirring constantly to avoid lumps. When mixture comes to a boil, lower heat and simmer for 8 to 10 minutes, or until the mixture starts to thicken, stirring constantly. Ladle 1/2 cup of the custard mixture into each cup, covering the fruit.

Whisk the cocoa powder into the remaining custard mixture. Blend thoroughly then distribute evenly among the 4 cups, carefully spooning the cocoa mixture over the other ingredients. Refrigerate for a minimum of 4 hours, or until the custard has set.

Invert the cups onto a shallow serving platter, so that the cherries are on the top. Garnish with the remaining peach slices. If desired, spoon several tablespoons of the peach juice over all.
Makes 4 servings.

Autumn:
MID-AUTUMN MOON FESTIVAL

id-Autumn Moon Festival occurs on the fifteenth day of the eighth month of
e Lunar Calendar. It marks the full moon, usually occurring in September or
ctober, when the harvest moon looms so large on the horizon. The round shape
mbolizes family, and Mid-Autumn Moon Festival marks the time for family
unions.

oon cakes come in hundreds of varieties, but this seasonal delicacy is tradition-
ly filled with the round orange yolk of an egg, reminiscent of the full moon.
milies take picnic baskets of moon cakes up mountainsides to watch the moon
e and recall previous times together.

Mid-Autumn
MOON FESTIVAL PICNIC

Shredded Pork Tofu
Stir-Fried Tofu with Bamboo Shoots
Apricot Walnut Moon Cakes
Pomelos
Guava Juice
Carambola (Star Fruit) Juice
Orange/Pineapple Juice

SHREDDED PORK TOFU

Made from soybeans, tofu is a wonderful source of calcium without the fat content of milk. Because the pieces are firm, they are easily eaten with wooden picks like hors d'oeuvres. Healthy and convenient, tofu is a favorite at picnics or family outings.

1 pound firm tofu
1/2 cup sesame oil
6 green onions
1 tablespoon cornstarch
1 tablespoon soy sauce
1 tablespoon fermented, salted black beans, optional (available at Oriental markets)
1 teaspoon minced chili pepper, or to taste
1/2 cup vegetable or chicken broth
2 tablespoons dried, shredded pork (available at Oriental markets)

Cut the tofu into bite-sized pieces. Place the tofu and oil in a wok. Stir-fry over a hot flame for 5 minutes. Slice the ends off the green onions and cut into 3-inch lengths. Add the onions to the wok and stir-fry for 3 minutes, or until the green onions are wilted and the tofu is heated through. Remove the tofu and onions from the heat and place in a serving bowl or covered container.

Mix the cornstarch and soy sauce. Add that mixture to the wok, along with the black beans, chili pepper, and broth, stirring constantly over medium heat. When the sauce is hot and thickened, pour over the tofu and green onions. Garnish all with the dried, shredded pork. Tofu may be eaten hot or cold. If eaten at a later time, keep it refrigerated.
Serves 4.

STIR-FRIED TOFU WITH BAMBOO SHOOTS

1 pound firm tofu
1 cup sesame oil
1/2 cup Chinese Refrigerated Pickles (see recipe page 97)
1/2 cup (4 ounces) sliced bamboo shoots (available at Oriental markets)
2 cloves garlic, minced
1 tablespoon cornstarch
1 tablespoon soy sauce
1/4 cup vegetable or chicken broth
1 teaspoon sesame seeds

Cut the tofu into bite-sized pieces. Deep-fry the pieces in sesame oil for 5 minutes, or until the tofu is crisp and golden brown. Drain the tofu and place in a serving bowl or covered container. Remove all but 2 tablespoons of the oil from the wok. (Reserve the remaining oil for another time.)

Stir-fry the pickled vegetables, bamboo shoots, and garlic in the oil for 2 to 3 minutes, or until the bamboo shoots are tender. Remove the vegetables, placing them with the tofu.

Combine the cornstarch and soy sauce. Add that mixture to the wok, along with the broth. Simmer over medium heat, stirring constantly, for 3 to 4 minutes, or until the sauce is hot and thickened. Pour the sauce over the tofu and vegetables. Sprinkle lightly with sesame seeds and serve. Tofu may be eaten hot or cold. If eaten at a later time, keep it refrigerated.
Serves 4.

APRICOT WALNUT MOON CAKES

FILLING:
1 1/2 cups chopped dried apricots
1 cup golden raisins
1 cup coconut flakes
1 1/2 cups coarsely chopped walnuts

CRUST:
4 cups all-purpose flour, sifted
1 tablespoon baking powder, sifted
1 teaspoon salt
4 large eggs
1 cup sugar
3/4 cup olive oil
2 teaspoons vanilla extract
2 tablespoons water

GLAZE:
2 eggs, beaten
1 tablespoon water

Cover the apricots with hot water. Allow the fruit to soften for 1 hour, then dice. Combine with the other ingredients and divide into 24 parts.

Combine the flour, baking powder, and salt. Whisk the eggs with the sugar until a ribbon is formed. Add the remaining crust ingredients and stir until a dough is formed. Pressing with your hands, form the dough into a ball, then into a rope 1 to 1 1/4 inches thick. Divide into 24 parts.

Preheat oven to 375°. Using your hands, flatten each piece to make a flat pancake (about 3 inches diameter). Place a portion of the filling inside. Roll this into a ball, making sure to seal in the filling. Again with your hands, flatten the top and bottom to form a round, 3-inch disk. Place on an ungreased baking sheet. Continue until all 24 moon cakes have been formed. Beat the eggs with the water. Lightly brush the cake tops and sides with the glaze, and bake for 30 minutes, or until done. Remove and allow cakes to cool before handling.
Makes 2 dozen moon cakes.

POMELOS

Pomelos, also spelled pummelos, look like over-sized grapefruit, some being as big as bowling balls. Thick skins account for much of their size, along with another thick layer of white pith. It isn't easy to peel pomelos, but it's worth the effort. The fruit is similar to grapefruit, but sweeter, chewier, and with a distinct flavor of its own.

To eat, slice off both ends. Score the pomelo, cutting deeply through the skin and pith. Peel away both skin and pith from the fruit's flesh. Section like a grapefruit, and eat it out of hand.

A Chinese myth suggests that water in which pomelo peels have been soaked drives away evil spirits. Whether that is so or not, pomelos are traditional fare on Mid-Autumn Moon Festival!

VEGETARIAN DINNER

Hot and Sour Soup
Five-Spice Tofu
Fluffy Rice
Baby Corn Vegetable Medley
Chinese Refrigerated Pickles
Crullers

The vast majority of Taiwanese are Buddhist, Taoist, or a mixture of the two religions. As a result, a very large portion of the population is vegetarian. The numerous vegetarian restaurants in Taiwan are a testament to that fact. However, meatless does not mean tasteless or monotonous. Vegetarian chefs are very creative, preparing hundreds, if not thousands, of meat look-alikes. Tofu is the blank canvas of Chinese cookery; its only limit is the imagination. Because it absorbs the flavor of other ingredients, tofu readily lends itself to any dish. Five-Spice Tofu a take-off on chicken. See if anyone notices the meatless difference!

The Best of Taiwanese Cuisine

HOT AND SOUR SOUP

Lily buds, also known as tiger-lily buds or golden needles, lend a touch of color, as well as a subtle musky flavor to soups and vegetarian dishes.

3 dried mushrooms
15 dried lily buds, optional (available at Oriental markets)
1 cup hot water
1 quart vegetable broth
1/2 cup (4 ounces) bamboo shoots, julienned
2 tablespoons cornstarch
3 tablespoons rice wine
1 tablespoon soy sauce
1/2 cup tofu, cut in 1/2-inch cubes
1 beaten egg
1/2 teaspoon ground white pepper, or to taste
1 tablespoon sesame oil
1/4 cup green onions, cut into 1-inch slivers
1/4 cup finely chopped cilantro

Plump the dried mushrooms and lily buds in hot water for 30 minutes. Cut off and discard any hard bits. Julienne the mushrooms.

Combine the mushrooms, lily buds, broth, and bamboo shoots in a 3-quart pot. Bring to a boil, then lower heat and simmer for 2 to 3 minutes. Combine the cornstarch, wine, and soy sauce. Add that mixture and the tofu to the soup and simmer for 2 to 3 minutes, or until the tofu is heated through. Whisk in the beaten egg. Add the pepper, oil, and onions. Ladle into bowls and garnish with chopped cilantro.
Makes 4 servings.

FIVE-SPICE TOFU

2 cups firm tofu, cut into 1/2-inch cubes
1/4 cup sesame oil
1/2 cup diagonally sliced celery
1/2 cup red bell pepper, cut into 1/4-inch strips
4 green onions, diagonally sliced
1 cup fresh pea pods, ends and veins removed
1 chili pepper, minced, optional
1/2 cup vegetable broth
1 1/2 tablespoons cornstarch
1 teaspoon five-spice powder (recipes follow)
2 tablespoons soy sauce
1 tablespoon raw or white sugar
1 tablespoon rice wine
3 to 4 cups hot fluffy rice

Stir-fry the tofu and oil over high flame in a wok for 2 to 3 minutes, or until the tofu is lightly browned. Remove the tofu with a slotted spoon; keep warm.

Add the celery, pepper, onions, pea pods, and chili pepper to the wok. Stir-fry over high heat for 3 to 4 minutes. Spoon the tofu back into the wok. Mix the broth and cornstarch. Add to the wok, along with the five-spice powder, soy sauce, sugar, and rice wine. Cook the mixture over low heat, stirring occasionally for 2 to 3 minutes, or until it thickens. Serve over the rice.
4 servings.

FIVE-SPICE POWDER—METHOD I

Five-spice powder is a very popular blend of spices available at Oriental markets, or you can make it yourself at home. It lends a somewhat sweet, pungent flavor and should be used in moderation. Add it to tofu, chicken, beef, or pork.

1/2 teaspoon crushed anise seed
1/2 teaspoon ground cinnamon
1/2 teaspoon crushed fennel
1/4 teaspoon ground cloves
1/4 teaspoon ground white pepper

Combine these ingredients thoroughly and store in an airtight container away from the sunlight.
Makes 2 teaspoons spice.

FIVE-SPICE POWDER—METHOD II

1/2 teaspoon crushed anise seed
1/2 teaspoon ground cinnamon
1/2 teaspoon crushed fennel
1/4 teaspoon ground ginger
1/4 teaspoon ground cloves

Combine these ingredients thoroughly and store in an airtight container away from the sunlight.
Makes 2 teaspoons spice.

FIVE-SPICE POWDER—METHOD III

12 whole star anise
12-inch whole cinnamon stick
2 tablespoons fennel seed
48 whole cloves
2 tablespoons black peppercorns

Combine the ingredients in a spice grinder or blender; grind to a fine texture. Store in an airtight container away from the sunlight.
Makes 1/2 cup spice.

BABY CORN VEGETABLE MEDLEY

1/2 cup sliced mushrooms
2 onions, peeled and quartered
2 stalks celery, diagonally sliced into 1/2-inch pieces
1 cup fresh green beans, trimmed and diagonally sliced into 1/2-inch pieces
1 tablespoon minced fresh ginger
2 garlic cloves, minced
1/4 cup sesame oil
1 tablespoon cornstarch
1 cup vegetable broth
2 tablespoons rice wine
1 tablespoon soy sauce, or to taste
1 cup green onions, diagonally sliced into 1/2-inch pieces
1 pound blanched baby corn or 1 can (15 ounces) baby corn

Combine the mushrooms, onions, celery, green beans, ginger, cloves, and oil in a wok. Stir-fry the vegetables for 3 minutes. Mix the cornstarch with the broth, wine, and soy sauce. Add to the vegetable mixture and stir for 3 minutes, or until the sauce bubbles. Add the green onions and baby corn, and simmer for 3 minutes, or until the vegetables are tender-crisp.
Serves 4.

CHINESE REFRIGERATED PICKLES

3 cups raw or light brown sugar
3 cups white vinegar
1 ¹/₂ cups water
1 teaspoon salt, or to taste
1 cup daikon or Chinese white radish, sliced into thin, 2-inch-long strips
(available at Oriental markets)
1 cup carrots, peeled and sliced into thin, 2-inch-long strips
1 cup celery, diagonally sliced into 1/2-inch pieces
1 cup green onions, trimmed and diagonally sliced into 1/4-inch pieces
1 cup julienned red bell pepper
1/2 cup thinly sliced fresh ginger

Combine the sugar, vinegar, water, and salt in a 3-quart saucepan. Bring to a boil, stirring to dissolve the sugar, and then allow to cool.

Add the remaining ingredients to 1 ¹/₂ quarts boiling water. Remove from heat, cover, and let stand for 3 minutes. Drain the vegetables thoroughly. Arrange on clean towels and air-dry for 2 hours.

Pack the vegetables into clean jars with tightly fitting lids. Pour the vinegar mixture over the vegetables, covering them but leaving 1/4-inch headspace. Seal the jars tightly and refrigerate. Use within 3 weeks.
Makes about 2 quarts pickles.

CONFUCIAN OR
TEACHER'S DAY
Luncheon

Honey-Roasted Pork Ribs
Pot-Stickers
Bok Choy
Honeydew Melon Slices
Peanut Brittle
Pistachios
Green Tea (see Tea Ceremony)

September 28 is always celebrated as Confucius' Birthday. It is also a holiday for teachers, with a welcome day off from school. Students traditionally give favorite teachers greeting cards or small gifts. In Taipei, Confucius' Birthday is celebrated at dawn with an elaborate ceremony at the Confucius Temple in the Tatung district.

Start your own tradition by inviting a favorite student or teacher to lunch.

The Best of Taiwanese Cuisine

HONEY-ROASTED PORK RIBS

8 pounds spareribs
2 quarts salted boiling water
1 cup honey
1/4 cup rice wine vinegar or white vinegar

Have the meat department crack the ribs in half lengthwise to form long strips. Simmer the ribs in salted, boiling water for 1 hour, or until tender. Drain thoroughly and thread onto long skewers for grilling. Combine the honey and vinegar. Brush half the piquant mixture over the ribs. Grill about 6 inches above the hot coals, turning and brushing often with the honey sauce, for about 25 minutes, or until richly glazed.
Serves 4.

POT-STICKERS

DOUGH

2 1/2 cups unsifted, all-purpose flour
1/2 teaspoon salt
1 tablespoon lard (traditional) or softened margarine
1 cup boiling water

Combine the ingredients and knead. Cover and allow to rest for 20 minutes.

FILLING

1 pound ground pork, cooked
1 cup finely chopped cabbage, all moisture squeezed out
2 tablespoons soy sauce
2 tablespoons rice wine
1 tablespoon sesame oil
1 tablespoon cornstarch
2 green onions, finely chopped
2 cloves garlic, minced
1 teaspoon minced fresh ginger
1/2 teaspoon ground white pepper
1 egg white
1/2 teaspoon raw or white sugar
1 teaspoon salt, or to taste
1 red chili pepper, minced, optional

Combine all the ingredients for the filling and mix well. Scoop out a teaspoon
of the rested dough and press it between your hands to form a 3-inch pancake.
Place about 1 teaspoon of the filling into the center of the pancake. Dampen
the edges of the dough and fold in half to form a crescent, being careful to
press out any air pockets.

STEAM-FRY

1/4 cup peanut or sesame oil
1 cup chicken broth

Heat the oil in a large frying pan. Arrange the dumplings and cook over medium heat for 5 minutes, or until golden brown. Pour the broth over the
dumplings, cover, and cook 3 to 5 minutes, or until most of the liquid is
absorbed.

DIPPING SAUCE

1/2 cup soy sauce
1 green onion, finely sliced
1 tablespoon finely chopped fresh ginger
1 tablespoon finely chopped garlic
1 tablespoon sesame oil

Combine all ingredients. Either drizzle over the dumplings or use as a dipping sauce.
Makes 1 cup sauce.

BOK CHOY

1 pound bok choy
1 clove garlic, minced
1 green onion, minced
1/4 teaspoon salt, or to taste
1/4 teaspoon ground pepper, or to taste
3 tablespoons sesame oil
1/4 cup water

Remove the outer, wilted leaves of the bok choy. Cut each into fourths and rinse well. Drain thoroughly. Combine all ingredients but the water in a wok and stir-fry for 3 minutes. Add the water, cover and steam for 5 minutes, or until the bok choy is tender. Do not overcook. Place on a heated platter and serve immediately.
Serves 4.

TEA CEREMONY

In Taiwan, the petite teapots are called Old-Man Teapots. The pots are only as large as apples, and the teacups not much larger than thimbles. The idea is to keep refilling each teacup, "toasting" to each other's health, and enjoying friendly conversation. The more teacups poured, the more interaction. The more interaction, the more fun.

First the teapot is warmed with boiling water, which also helps to cleanse any remaining tea flavor. The pot is filled to the brim with tight, dry tea leaves, the finest the host can afford.

Boiling water is poured into and over the teapot to wash away any impurities. The lid is replaced, and more boiling water is poured over all. This helps seal in the heat, allowing the tea leaves to swell more rapidly and release their flavor.

Two teacups are placed at each setting. The taller one is for sniffing, and the other is for drinking. Never drink from the snifter teacup. The tea is poured into the snifter; the narrow shape of the snifter enhances the aroma. Breathe in the fragrance. Then pour the tea into the smaller, wider teacup and savor the unique flavor.

Traditionally the teacups must be held with both hands, and drinking to quench one's thirst is not socially acceptable. Instead, "toast" the health of the other tea drinkers, holding up the small cup in salute.

Wulong (Black Dragon) tea is the favorite for tea ceremonies. Half fermented, it contains both the mellow flavor of black tea and the refreshing sweetness of green tea.

Any time is the right time for tea, but an afternoon tea is a particularly good moment to share this time-honored ceremony with friends.

The Best of Taiwanese Cuisine

AFTERNOON TEA

Wulong Tea
Roasted Cashews
Roasted Pistachios
Roasted Buffalo Beans (available at Oriental markets)
Watermelon Seeds (available at Oriental markets)
Sesame Lace Cookies
Peanut Brittle
Almond Cookies

No one can resist an afternoon tea party, especially when it is traditional Chinese style! Serve the various nuts, seeds, and beans in small rice bowls for munching. Experiment with several of the exotic flavors of watermelon seeds. Put a small plate beside the two teacups at each place setting. (Be sure to set a rice bowl at each place setting for discarded shells.) Serve the candy, peanut brittle, and cookies on elegant platters. For a centerpiece, arrange white and pink baby carnations, offset with fragrant dill fronds.

SESAME LACE COOKIES

1 cup all-purpose flour
1/2 teaspoon baking powder
1/2 teaspoon salt, or to taste
1/4 cup raw or white sugar
1/4 cup dark corn syrup
1/4 cup margarine, softened
1 tablespoon water, or as needed
1/4 cup sesame seeds
1 teaspoon sesame oil

Preheat oven to 325°. Sift the flour, baking powder, and salt. Mix the sugar, corn syrup, and margarine in a saucepan. Stir constantly and, if necessary, add a little water to prevent scorching. Bring to a boil, then lower heat and cook for 4 to 5 minutes, stirring often. Cool for 3 to 5 minutes. Gradually stir the flour mixture into the syrup. Fold in the sesame seeds and mix well.

Lightly grease cookie sheet with sesame oil. Scoop out 1/4 teaspoon mixture and drop on cookie sheet, allowing 3 inches between cookies. Dough will flatten as it bakes, bubbles, and forms a lacy pattern. Bake for 8 to 10 minutes, or until golden brown. Be careful not to scorch. Cool before handling. Remove to racks to harden and cool completely.
Makes about 12 dozen cookies.

PEANUT BRITTLE

For a crispier brittle, use 1 less tablespoon butter: the less butter, the harder the candy.

1/2 teaspoon sesame oil
1 1/2 cups raw or white sugar
1/2 cup honey
1/2 cup butter, softened
1/2 pound peanuts

Line a cookie sheet with baking parchment, to which sesame oil has been applied

Mix the sugar and honey over low heat. Add the butter, stirring constantly until thoroughly blended. Fold in the peanuts. Working quickly to prevent the mixture from hardening prematurely, use a metal spatula to spread the mixture evenly on the lined cookie sheet. When the brittle has cooled enough to handle, but before it has hardened completely, cut it into a diamond-shaped pattern. Cut the brittle diagonally in one direction. Next cut it to parallel the narrow edge of the cookie sheet.

Makes 5 dozen pieces.

ALMOND COOKIES

1 ¹/₄ cups margarine
2 ¹/₂ cups sifted, all-purpose flour
1 teaspoon baking powder
1 ¹/₂ cups raw or white sugar
1 teaspoon almond extract
2 eggs, beaten
1 tablespoon water, or as needed
24 to 30 blanched whole almonds

Preheat oven to 375°. Cut the margarine into the flour, baking powder, and sugar until the mixture crumbles. Add the almond extract, beaten eggs, and enough water to the flour mixture to form a soft dough. Knead lightly to blend and allow to rest for 5 to 10 minutes.

Roll the dough into 1 ¹/₂-inch balls. Press between your hands to form 1/2-inch-thick pancakes. Press an almond in the center of each. Arrange on floured cookie sheets. Bake for 5 minutes. Lower the temperature to 300° and bake for another 7 to 8 minutes or until the cookies are golden brown at the edges.

Makes 2 to 2 ¹/₂ dozen cookies.

SUNDAY CHICKEN DINNER
—Chinese Style

Creamy Corn Soup
Smoked Tea Chicken
Mandarin Pancakes
Plum Sauce
Shiitake Mushrooms and Pea Pods
Braised Oriental Eggplant
Wulong Tea
Peanut Crescents

Sunday is Sunday, whether in the East or West. It is a day to spend with the family, away from the stress of the office, over a leisurely meal. Start the dinner with Creamy Corn Soup, true comfort food with its velvety texture. Sample the melt-in-your-mouth-tender Smoked Tea Chicken with Mandarin Pancakes, reminiscent of Beijing Duck, but with a unique flavor of its own. Round out the repast with Shiitake Mushrooms and Pea Pods and Braised Oriental Eggplant. Relax over Wulong Tea, nibbling on Peanut Crescents, while enjoying good company and conversation.

CREAMY CORN SOUP

2 large fresh ears corn,
   OR 1 can (8 3/4 ounces) cream-style corn
3 cups chicken broth
1 teaspoon salt, or to taste
1/4 teaspoon ground white pepper, or to taste
1 tablespoon cornstarch
2 tablespoons water
2 egg whites, beaten
2 tablespoons milk
1/4 cup finely chopped ham
1/4 cup fresh cilantro leaves

Husk the fresh corn. Using a sharp knife, very carefully slice the corn kernels off the cob, taking care not to cut into the kernels or let their juice escape. Add to a 2-quart pot, along with the broth, salt, and pepper. Bring to a boil. Combine the cornstarch and water. Gradually pour into the soup, stirring constantly, until the soup has thickened. Turn off the heat. Combine the beaten egg whites and milk. Fold into the soup and immediately ladle into 4 bowls. Garnish with a sprinkling of ham bits and cilantro leaves.
Serves 4.

SMOKED TEA CHICKEN

Be very careful when using Szechwan peppercorns. Wear rubber gloves to crush the peppercorns or rub the marinade on the chicken, be sure not to touch your eyes or mouth, and wash your hands when finished. *Yes, Mother.*

MARINADE
3 tablespoons minced fresh ginger
2 tablespoons rice wine
2 tablespoons soy sauce
2 tablespoons raw or white sugar
2 green onions, sliced into 1-inch slivers
1 teaspoon salt, or to taste
1 teaspoon ten-spice powder (see recipe page 117)
1 teaspoon coarsely crushed Szechwan or black peppercorns

1 (3 to 4-pound) broiler/fryer chicken

SMOKING MIXTURE
1/3 cup black tea leaves
1/3 cup dark brown sugar
1/3 cup uncooked long-grain rice
2 teaspoons grated orange peel (from washed, organic orange)

6 Green Onion Chrysanthemums (recipe follows page 110)
Mandarin Pancakes (recipe follows page 110)
Plum Sauce (recipe follows page 111)
4 green onions, sliced into 1-inch slivers

Combine all the marinade ingredients. Wearing rubber gloves, rub the chicken inside and out with the marinade. Cover, refrigerate, and allow flavors to marry overnight, or at least for 8 hours.

Place chicken, breast side up, on rack in a large pot or wok. Add 1 ¹/₂ inches water, cover, and bring to a boil. Lower heat and steam for 45 minutes, or until a meat thermometer placed in the chicken's thigh registers 185°. Remove from heat. When chicken is cool enough to handle, lift from rack, draining off any juices in cavity.

Line a large wok and lid with aluminum foil. (Do not use an electric wok or a nonstick finish.) Combine all the ingredients of the smoking mixture, and place on bottom of the foil-lined wok. Set rack on top, and arrange chicken breast side up on rack. Cover with the foil-lined lid.

Cook for 2 minutes over high heat. Turn off the heat and let stand for 5 minutes. Do not remove cover or peek. Repeat twice more. After the third smoking, leave covered for 30 minutes more, allowing smoke to subside. When cool enough to handle, remove the chicken and discard the smoking mixture.

Slice the chicken and arrange on a heated platter. Garnish with green onion chrysanthemums. Serve as you would Beijing Duck. Place a slice of chicken on a mandarin pancake. Top with sauce and slivered onions and eat out of hand. **Serves 6 to 8.**

GREEN ONION CHRYSANTHEMUMS

6 green onions
1 cup cold water
12 ice cubes

To make green onion chrysanthemums, trim off the white bulbs. Reserve for another use. Cut into 6-inch lengths. Using sharp kitchen shears, cut both tips, making 6 to 8 narrow cuts almost to the middle of the green onion, leaving long fringe at both ends. Leave about 1/2 inch uncut in the center. Place onions in ice water, and the tips will flare out like chrysanthemums. Use as garnishes for elegant presentations.

To make tight green onion curls, follow the directions above, but instead of 6-inch lengths, cut the green onions into 4-inch lengths.

MANDARIN PANCAKES

Mandarin Pancakes are available at Oriental markets, but nothing tastes as good as the homemade variety. Only needing 3 ingredients, the recipe is easy. Don't be put off by the directions. They only *look* difficult. After you have made Mandarin Pancakes once or twice, they will seem effortless.

3 cups sifted, all-purpose flour
1 cup plus 1 tablespoon boiling water
3 to 4 tablespoons sesame oil

Sift flour into a large mixing bowl. Make a well in the center. Add the boiling water, and mix with a spoon. When mixture is crumbly, press into a ball. Knead the dough on a lightly floured surface for 5 minutes, or until it has a satin sheen. Cover and leave for 30 minutes.

Roll the dough between your palms into a 15-inch-long rope. Cut into 15 equal pieces. Cover dough. Cut each piece in half and roll into a 3-inch circle on a lightly floured surface. Brush the top with a little sesame oil. Do the same with the other half. Press the 2 pancakes together, oil side in, and roll both simultaneously into 6- to 7-inch circles. Keep rolled pancakes covered. Repeat for the remaining dough.

Using a nonstick skillet, fry the pancakes in only a drop or two of oil. Cook 1 pair at a time, separated, turning every 30 seconds, for 1 to 2 minutes, or until pancakes are dry to the touch and lightly brown. (Cooked pancakes may be frozen in airtight plastic bags and reheated in the microwave.)

Serve warm, folded into triangular quarters.
Makes 30 pancakes.

PLUM SAUCE

1 cup plum jelly
1/2 cup finely chopped chutney
1 tablespoon raw or white sugar
1 teaspoon rice wine vinegar

Combine the ingredients in a small sauce pan and heat over low flame for 1 to 2 minutes, or until the sugar and jelly dissolve. Chill before serving.
Makes 1 ¹/₂ cups sauce.

SHIITAKE MUSHROOMS AND PEA PODS

Asians elevate vegetable garnishes to an art form. If you have extra time, try trimming the carrots to resemble wings. Sliced a peeled carrot lengthwise. Quarter the 2 halves width-wise. Make 3 wide slices from each of the halved quarters, creating about 24 carrot slices. Round the tips of the slices. Notch the ends to resemble feathered wings. (No need to waste the leftover pieces. Chop them finely and add to the dish.) Who said carrots were ho-hum?

1/2 pound shiitake mushrooms, sliced
1/2 pound fresh pea pods, ends and veins removed
1 cup peeled, sliced carrots
1 clove garlic, minced
1 green onion, minced
1/4 teaspoon salt, or to taste
1/4 teaspoon ground pepper, or to taste
3 tablespoons sesame oil
1/4 cup water

Combine all ingredients but the water in a wok and stir-fry for 3 minutes. Add the water, cover and steam for 5 to 7 minutes, or until the vegetables are tender. Do not overcook.
Place on a heated platter
and serve immediately.
Serves 4.

The Best of Taiwanese Cuisine

BRAISED ORIENTAL EGGPLANT

Oriental eggplants are long, slender eggplants that resemble purple bananas more than eggs. Their flavor is subtle but distinctive.

1 pound Oriental eggplant
2 cups heavily salted water (salt retains the purple color)
2 star anise seeds
3 green onions, finely chopped
1/2 tablespoon finely chopped fresh ginger
2 cloves garlic, minced
1/4 cup sesame oil
1 tablespoon soy sauce
1 tablespoon rice wine
1 tablespoon raw or white sugar

Slice the eggplants width-wise into bite-sized pieces. Parboil them in the salted water and star anise seeds for 5 minutes. Drain and combine with the remaining ingredients in a wok. Stir-fry over a medium flame for 5 minutes, or until tender. **Serves 4.**

PEANUT CRESCENTS

If only square wonton wrappers are available, fold in half and trim with scissors to make crescents or leave as is for triangular-shaped pastries.

1 cup finely chopped salted peanuts
1 cup raw or light brown sugar
1/2 cup flaked coconut
48 (1 pound) 3-inch round wonton wrappers (see recipe page 40)
   (available at Oriental markets)
1 beaten egg
3 cups peanut or vegetable oil for deep-frying

Combine the peanuts, sugar, and coconut. Spoon 1 teaspoon filling into the center of each wonton. Fold the wontons in half. Moisten the edges with beaten egg and pinch to seal. Deep-fry several at a time in oil to a golden brown, turning once.
Makes 4 dozen.

DOUBLE-TEN CELEBRATION

Asparagus Vinaigrette
Ginger Beef
Chinese Vermicelli
Sweet and Sour Mustard Greens
Almond Silk Soup
Papaya Wedges and Strawberries

Double Ten, or the tenth day of the tenth month, is Taiwan's Independence Day. A national holiday, businesses are closed. Everyone has the day off to watch the parade in front of the Presidential Building, stroll through Chiang Kai-shek park, study the floats constructed of native flowers, enjoy the performances of the various aborigine, dragon, and lion dances, then gaze up at the splendid fireworks at dusk. The day ends late, and everyone is ready to relax over an elegant (but completely make-ahead) dinner.

ASPARAGUS VINAIGRETTE

1 pound young asparagus
1 tablespoon rice wine
1 tablespoon dark soy sauce
1 tablespoon sesame oil
1 tablespoon raw or dark brown sugar

Break off the hard root ends of the asparagus and discard. Slice diagonally into 1 ¹/₂-inch lengths. Blanch the asparagus in boiling water for 1 minute. Drain and rinse in cold water. Combine the remaining ingredients and toss lightly with the asparagus. Serve chilled.
Makes 4 servings.

GINGER BEEF

Dried black mushrooms, with caps up to 3 inches wide, impart a rich, distinctive flavor. Always soak in hot water before using, and then thinly slice.

1 pound beef flank steak

MARINADE
3 tablespoons beef broth
2 tablespoons soy sauce
1 tablespoon rice wine
1/2 cup minced fresh ginger
1 tablespoon Ten-Spice Powder (recipe follows)

SAUCE
2 tablespoons cornstarch
2 tablespoons oyster sauce (prepared or see recipe page 82)
1/2 cup beef broth

SEASONINGS
6 dried black mushrooms
1 (8 1/2-ounce) can bamboo shoots
1/2 cup green onions, cut diagonally into 1-inch pieces
2 cloves garlic, minced
1 teaspoon raw or white sugar
1/2 teaspoon salt, or to taste
1 tablespoon beef broth
4 tablespoons peanut or vegetable oil

Slice flank steak into very thin slices (1/8 inch) across the grain. Combine all the marinade ingredients, and marinate overnight, or at least for 2 hours. Mix the sauce ingredients and set aside.

Stem the mushrooms and thinly slice the caps into strips. Julienne the bamboo shoots. Stir-fry the mushrooms, green onions, and seasonings in 2 tablespoons of the oil for 1 minute. Set aside. Remove the beef from the marinade and drain. Add the remaining 2 tablespoons of oil and the beef to the wok. Stir-fry the meat for 7 to 9 minutes, or until the beef is tender. Add the sauce and stir 2 minutes, or until thickened. Fold in the vegetables and seasonings. Stir-fry for 3 minutes, or until well mixed and heated through.
Serves 4.

TEN-SPICE POWDER

Szechwan pepper is reddish-brown in color, with a pungent fragrance and a potent flavor. Use in moderation. Because of a delayed reaction to the flavor, taste buds may respond to its heat too late, after too much pepper has been added. Be very cautious when handling Szechwan peppercorns. Wear gloves when crushing them, avoid touching your eyes or mouth, and wash your hands when finished.

2 tablespoons coarsely crushed Szechwan peppercorns
2 tablespoons fennel seeds
12 whole star anise, snapped into points
1 tablespoon coriander seeds
1 teaspoon cumin seeds
1 teaspoon whole cloves
1 teaspoon black peppercorns
1/2 teaspoon ground turmeric
1/2 teaspoon ground cinnamon
1/4 teaspoon ground ginger

Combine all the ingredients except the turmeric, cinnamon, and ginger in a dry nonstick skillet. Stirring constantly with a wooden spoon, toast over low flame for 2 to 3 minutes, or until the spices release their fragrance. Whisk in the remaining ingredients and remove from heat. Transfer to a spice grinder or blender, and grind to a fine texture. Store in an airtight container away from the sunlight.
Makes 1 cup spice.

CHINESE VERMICELLI

4 cups cooked Chinese vermicelli

Chinese vermicelli, also known as transparent or cellophane noodles, are unusually fine noodles made from mung beans. They are colorless and almost tasteless, but they quickly absorb the flavors of the food with which they are prepared. What makes them unique is their pliable and elastic texture, the perfect complement to the firm texture of Ginger Beef. Chinese vermicelli can be simmered, steamed, deep-fried, or used in stir-fry dishes. Follow the package's instructions for preparation.

SWEET AND SOUR MUSTARD GREENS

1 pound mustard greens, washed and trimmed
12 grape or cherry tomatoes, rinsed and halved
1/2 cup peanut or vegetable oil
1/4 teaspoon ground white pepper, or to taste
1 tablespoon sesame seeds

SAUCE
3 tablespoons soy sauce
3 tablespoons rice wine vinegar
3 tablespoons raw or white sugar
2 tablespoons cornstarch

Combine the greens, tomatoes, oil, and pepper in a wok. Stir-fry over high heat for 2 to 3 minutes, or until tender crisp. Blend the sauce ingredients, and add to the greens mixture. Stir-fry all for another 1 to 2 minutes, or until the sauce begins to thicken. Remove to a heated platter. Sprinkle with sesame seeds to garnish.
Serves 4.

ALMOND SILK SOUP

1/2 cup cooked rice
1/2 cup almond paste
2 cups water
2 cups milk
1 tablespoon raw or white sugar
1/2 teaspoon almond extract
4 whole almonds

Blend the rice, almond paste, and water in a blender, using the pulse speed, until smooth. Pour into a saucepan, and add the milk and sugar. The soup may be prepared in advance up to this point. Heat or reheat thoroughly, but do not boil. Whisk in the almond extract, and serve immediately. Spoon into 4 rice or dessert bowls, garnishing each bowl with an almond.
Serves 4.

MAHJONG NIGHT
Dinner for Four

Fan-Shaped Chicken
Steak and Eggs Fried Rice
Stir-Fried Zucchini
Tapioca Pudding
Mandarin Orange Wedges

Many Chinese enjoy a rousing game of Mahjong. Like bridge or poker clubs in the United States, many Taiwanese have weekly Mahjong games with regular foursomes. Following an afternoon game or preceding an evening game, the players enjoy a hearty dinner of crunchy chicken and fried rice.

FAN-SHAPED CHICKEN

4 chicken breasts, each with wing attached
2 tablespoons rice wine
1/2 teaspoon salt
2 egg whites, beaten
1 cup dry breadcrumbs
3 cups peanut or vegetable oil for deep-frying

Skin and bone each chicken breast, leaving the wing attached. Cut partially through the thickest parts of each breast to form a fan shape. Use a mallet to tenderize and further flatten each breast, shaping it into a fan, leaving the wing tip pointing upwards. Marinate in the wine and salt for 15 minutes. Drain and brush with the egg whites. Dredge in the breadcrumbs and deep-fry until done to a golden brown crispness. Serve wing-side up on a heated platter. **Serves 4.**

STEAK AND EGGS FRIED RICE

Fried rice is never made the same way twice. It is the consummate usage for left-overs. Don't feel obligated to follow the recipe exactly. Use whatever is on hand. Chop up almost any bit of meat, fish, or vegetable, and add it to the recipe. In Taiwan, even the rice is leftover from the previous day!

3 eggs, lightly beaten
1/2 teaspoon salt, or to taste
1/4 teaspoon ground white pepper, or to taste
3 tablespoons peanut or vegetable oil, divided
1 clove garlic, minced
4 green onions, thinly sliced
1/4 cup diced mushrooms
1 tablespoon soy sauce, or to taste
4 ounces cooked flank steak, finely chopped
4 cups cooked long-grain rice
1 tablespoon fresh cilantro leaves

Add the eggs, salt, and pepper to 1 tablespoon oil in a hot wok. Cook 1 to 2 minutes over medium heat, or until eggs set. Remove eggs and chop coarsely. Set aside.

Combine the remaining 2 tablespoons oil, garlic, onions, mushrooms, and soy sauce in the wok. Stir-fry over medium heat for 2 to 3 minutes. Add the steak and rice. Stir-fry for 2 to 3 minutes, or until heated through, adding a tablespoon of water if mixture begins to stick to the wok. Blend in the cooked eggs and serve at once. Garnish with cilantro leaves.
Serves 4.

ALTERNATE INGREDIENTS:

Add bits of any cut of beef, pork, bacon, ham, lamb, chicken, duck, tofu, shrimp, clams, fish, crabmeat, lobster, scallops, squid, eggs, green pepper, red pepper, zucchini, napa cabbage, peas, pea pods, celery, corn, carrots, onions, leeks, chives, bean sprouts, bamboo shoots, grated ginger, or chili pepper.

STIR-FRIED ZUCCHINI

2 medium (1 1/2 to 2 pounds) zucchini
1 clove garlic, minced
1/2 teaspoon minced ginger
2 tablespoons peanut or vegetable oil
1/2 teaspoon salt, or to taste
1/4 teaspoon ground white pepper, or to taste
1/2 cup chicken broth

Trim, wash, and slice the zucchini. Stir-fry the garlic and ginger in the oil for 1 minute. Add the zucchini, salt, and pepper, and stir-fry for 1 to 2 minutes. Pour in the broth. Cover and simmer over low heat for 5 to 6 minutes, or until the zucchini is tender. Serve immediately.
Serves 4.

TAPIOCA PUDDING

Prepare the tapioca pudding according to the directions on the package. Instead of vanilla extract, use almond extract. When given the option of whipping the egg whites or not, do whip the egg whites into stiff peaks, and fold into the hot pudding mixture. Serve hot with mandarin orange wedges.

Index

0295